Diabetic Alert Dog Training Steps

Training Your Pet To Be Your Partner

By Libby Rockaway

M.D. Dogs Inc's

Diabetic Alert Dog Training Steps
Training Your Pet To Be Your Partner

By Libby Rockaway

M.D. Dogs Incorporated

Diabetic Alert Dog Training Steps
www.MDdogs.org

Copyright © 2021 by Libby Rockaway

All rights reserved.

No part of this book may be used or reproduced in any manner whatsoever without written permission, except in the case of brief quotations embodied in critical articles and reviews and solely personal use on a home printer. All other application permissions must be granted in writing by contacting the author at: MDdogsInc@gmail.com

Diabetic Alert Dog Training Steps contains a variety of training recommendations for your dog. While caution has been taken to give safe recommendations, it is impossible to predict an individual dog's reaction to the recommended handling or training. A Service Dog is an animal and is not intended to replace any medical care or any devices provided by medical professionals. A Diabetic Alert Service Dog is never 100% accurate and should never replace regular blood glucose level checking.

Neither the author, Libby Rockaway, nor M.D. Dogs Incorporated accepts liability for any mental, financial, or physical harm that arises from the following advice, techniques, or procedures in this book. Readers should use personal judgment when applying the recommendations of this text.

SECOND EDITION

ISBN: 978-0-578-55807-3
Published by LLL Publishing, Nicholasville, Kentucky, USA

Cover Photo: Jeannie Francis Photography
Interior Layout: Laura Reynolds
Interior Art: Ibis Lagumbay Art Studio

Contents

About this Book	7	Scent Games	89
About the Author	8	Socialization & Public Access	93
Introduction	9	Example Timeline	97
Before You Begin	11	Stress Signals	98
Daily Training Schedule	18	Public Access Guidelines	101
Training - Week 1	19	MD Dogs Public Access Test	104
Training - Week 2	20	Flying with your Service Dog	114
Training - Week 3	21	School with Your Service Dog	117
Training - Week 4	22	Work with Your Service Dog	120
Choosing Your Dog	23	"Graduating" Your DAD	121
Ideal Puppy Traits	29	Washing Out A DAD in Training	122
Puppy Temperament Test	30	Acknowledgements	125
Choosing an Adult Dog	39	Resources	129
Ideal Adult Dog Traits	40	Financial Estimate	130
Scent Training Steps	41	United States Service Dog Laws	131
Scent Training Pointers	72	Records	131
False Alerts	74	Exposure List	134
Walking Alerts	78	Scent Training Checklist	136
Night Alerts	80	Alert Log	138
Bringsel Training	82	Training Log	142

Thank you to Mr. William Levy for consistent encouragement and mentorship, whose support made M.D. Dogs Inc become a reality.

M.D. Dogs Inc is supported solely through donations. If you find M.D. Dogs resources beneficial, please consider donating at www.MDdogs.org to help us contine to provide resources and further the field of medical detection dogs.

About

About this Book

The M.D. Dogs book, *Diabetic Alert Dog Training Steps*, and video series contain instructions for how to train a Diabetic Alert Dog (DAD). The primary purpose of these resources is to teach type 1 diabetics or their caregivers to train their own DADs. An additional goal is to bring transparency to the field of DADs. While the M.D. Dogs method is not the only way to train a DAD, my hope is that it will give everyone a better understanding of how and why DADs work, and aid in removing the mystery surrounding them.

This book is intended to accompany the M.D. Dogs video series as well as *Puppy Steps: Practical training for your new best friend*. Some material will be repeated, but to understand the training fully it is suggested that you utilize all three materials. *Puppy Steps* can be found on Amazon.com and the free training videos are on MDdogs.org. It is also suggested that you utilize the logs in this workbook (under "Resources") to record your dog's training in case documentation is ever required.

Lastly, M.D. Dogs highly recommends finding a local trainer to assist you in the training of your DAD, in addition to utilizing the resources provided. A local trainer can help you throughout the process - ensuring you are on the right path, answering any questions you have along the way, and confirming when your dog's behavior is that of a service dog.

About

About the Author

Libby Rockaway has transparentized the field of Diabetic Alert Dogs through her succinct and systematic training process and the publishing of her book, *Diabetic Alert Dog Training Steps: Training Your Pet To Be Your Partner.*

As a professional pet dog trainer for clients throughout the world, Libby gained years of experience training dogs with all manner of drive and personality. After solidifying her puppy training methods, she wrote *Puppy Steps: Practical Training for Your New Best Friend* as a straightforward guide to raising a well behaved puppy. *Puppy Steps* is the foundation of all her training.

Training pet dogs eventually led Libby to her passion — training service dogs. Since 2013, she has focused on Diabetic Alert Dogs, matching her trained dogs with children with type 1 diabetes through her business, LLLeashes LLC. Over the course of this training she developed a step-by-step method for teaching scent detection, as well as techniques to quickly grow the communication and relationship between the dog and handler.

Her successes led to families seeking Libby out for help in training their own Diabetic Alert Dogs. Realizing that the demand for trained service dogs far outstrips the supply and many families are capable of self-training, Libby founded M.D. Dogs Incorporated, a non-profit dedicated to providing resources, standards, and research for training Medical Detection Dogs.

Libby's credentials include both a Bachelor of Arts in Cognitive Neuroscience and a Master of Science in Nonprofit Leadership from the University of Pennsylvania, as well as a Master of Science in Animal Behaviour and Welfare from Queen's University Belfast. She is a member of the Association of Professional Dog Trainers and the International Association of Canine Professionals, and has attended numerous conferences on Diabetic Alert Dog training, canine cognition, working dogs, and diabetes. In 2016, Libby performed research on canine training and behavior, which she presented at the 2018 PennVet Working Dog Conference.

Libby's goal for both LLLeashes LLC and M.D. Dogs Incorporated is to provide individuals the opportunity and tools to have their own service dogs, helping keep them safe and healthy until there is a cure.

More information can be found at MDdogs.org or MD Dogs Inc on Facebook and Instagram.

Introduction

Introduction

To start your dog off on the right paw, prior to beginning training, please read through this book in its entirety, create a training plan, and purchase *Puppy Steps* by Libby Rockaway (which can be found on Amazon).

Female pronouns are used throughout this book to refer to the dog in training. DADs can be either males or females and there are no results showing that one gender is more successful than the other. The use of a female pronoun is solely to avoid extraneous words.

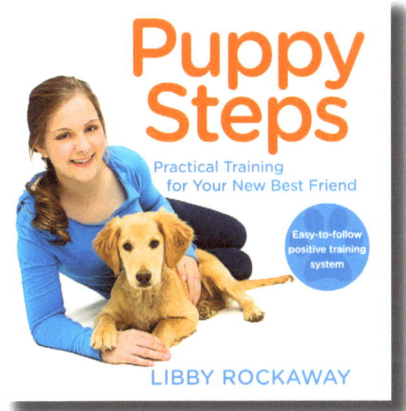

If you will be training a puppy, you may begin both scent and obedience training as young as 8 weeks of age. (A puppy should not be separated from its siblings prior to 8 weeks). Scent training and obedience training are intended to be taught simultaneously - there is no benefit to waiting until a dog has achieved a certian level of obedience prior to beginning scent training. You can alternate between scent and obedience training within one training session or you can alternate entire training sessions dedicated to scent training or obedience.

Initially, training sessions should be less than 5 minutes, a few times each day. As your puppy matures, you can increase the duration of sessions.

If you are training an adult dog and intend to train her for public access, have a local service dog trainer evaluate your dog first to determine if she has the potential to become a service dog. If the trainer agrees that your dog is a good service dog candidate, you can begin training. While it is always okay to train in very short sessions, adults have longer attention spans so they can work for a little longer than a puppy's 5 minute maximum. If your dog's body langauge shows your dog is becoming bored, or if she becomes unsuccessful, always end the session.

Before implementing any scent training, always check your blood sugar and ensure you are in range unless specifically practicing a live blood sugar alert.

DAD training requires precision and intentionality. This means that when you mark and reward (see *Puppy Steps* for definition), it needs to be at the exact right moment. Additionally, ensure all your verbal cues and hand motions are intentional.

Introduction

When you give a command, say "Name, Command". For example, "Filly, Sit". Do not say "Sit, Siiiiit, Sit!". Hand signals and gestures should be crisp as well. If you'd like to use hand signals in addition to verbal commands (which I recommend as sometimes in public you will not want to verbally tell your dog to lie down, sit, stay, etc.), decide what the hand signal will be, then make sure every time you practice with your dog you use the same exact gesture.

Dogs are excellent at reading our body language. This can cause an issue in training because we need DADs to act independently of our actions. If each time we play a scent game I stare at the correct blood sugar sample container, my dog will find the low sample every time, but it will be due to me staring at it rather than her detecting the scent. Because of this, she may never live alert. To prevent this, frequently video your training sessions so that you can see your own mannerisms. Look for behaviors that could be cuing your dog to perform a certain way or could confuse your dog. Then consciously avoid those behaviors in the future.

Not every dog is capable of being a service dog. It is estimated that only 1 in 4 or even as low as 1 in 8 dogs successfully complete their training as service dogs. If at any point you are unsure whether your dog is able to be a Diabetic Alert Dog, talk to a local service dog trainer and allow them to objectively evaluate your dog.

Training a DAD takes time and patience. Do not rush the process, but practice frequently. With persistence and consistency, your dog can be alerting to your out of range blood sugars within a few weeks to a few months and will help keep you safe and healthy for years to come.

I wish you the best!

Libby Rockaway

Shopping List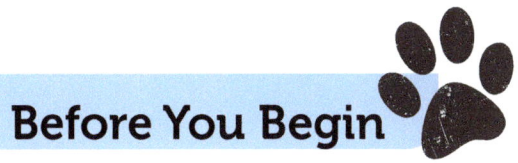

Before You Begin

The items with an asterisk indicate the items that should be purchased prior to any training. The supplies for scent samples are enough to make 10 samples, which is the suggested minimum before beginning training.

ITEM	Suggested Source:
☐ *Scent samples	
☐ (10) Dental rolls or gauze	Amazon
☐ (10) 5ml plastic graduated vials or pill bags	Amazon
☐ (1) Unused glass canning jar	Amazon
☐ Scent wheel	See Page 17
☐ (1) 18" circular wood piece	Hardware Store
☐ (1) Lazy susan	Hardware Store
☐ (1) 2" threaded pvc cap	Hardware Store
☐ (1) 2" pvc snap in drain	Hardware Store
☐ (8) Wood screws	Hardware Store
☐ *(3) ½ Ounce metal tins	Amazon
☐ *Low value treats (e.g. dog food)	Pet store
☐ *Medium value treats (e.g. Zuke's)	Pet store
☐ *High value treats (e.g. meat/cheese)	Grocery store
☐ Service dog vest	ActiveDogs.com
☐ *Kennel (plastic or wire)	Pet store
☐ *Toys	Pet store
☐ Place (blanket or mat)	Walmart
☐ *6 foot flat leash	Pet store
☐ *Buckle collar	Pet store
☐ Clicker (optional)	Pet store
☐ Dog cot (optional)	Kuranda.com

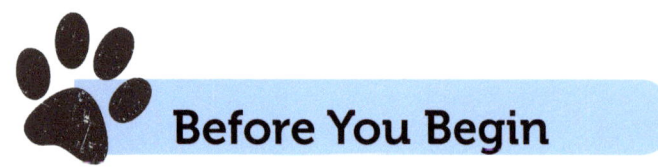

Before You Begin

Training a puppy to be a Diabetic Alert Dog is not easy nor linear! Whether a professional trainer or a self-trainer, a trainer's enthusiasm for the dog's potential as a Diabetic Alert Dog will tend to oscillate as the dog progresses. If you are bringing a puppy home with the goal of training her to be a Diabetic Alert Dog, know from the start that there will be more ups and downs than you can remember. It will be worth it in the end without a doubt, but throughout the process it is very normal to have days of utter excitement and confidence, followed by days of disappointment and doubts.

When searching for a puppy you are at a relatively high point - excited, perhaps a little nervous, and looking forward to the future! The puppy comes home and everyone is ecstatic with this new, innocent and adorable family member! A few days in though, this family member has become a lot of work - needing outside constantly, never being able to be left alone, preventing you from getting any sleep, and not understanding that human flesh is not an acceptable chew toy. But pretty soon you will get into a routine and develop a new normal. Around this time, your pup will also really start to accelerate her learning - she has become comfortable with her new home and wow, is she smart! You are back up to an enthusiasm high point - your pup is going to be an incredible Diabetic Alert Dog!

But then, the dreaded adolescence hits you. Your little perfect pup who used to be so responsive and willing to please, somehow turned into an opinionated and independent teenager seemingly overnight! This typically occurs around 5-8 months of age and you begin to wonder why you spent all that time training her, when she appears to have forgotten it all in the blink of an eye. Adolescence lasts a few months typically and can be exhausting. It requires more supervising, returning to the basics, and practicing your patience. But it does end, I promise!

After a rough month or two of adolescence, you begin to see glimpses of a mature adult dog every once in a while - these glimpses give hope! Slowly but surely she inches her way out of adolescence and you start to have a dog who is becoming more reliable, steady, and responsive. Unlike entering adolescence, exiting adolescence doesn't happen overnight, but you'll notice it over time as you are able to spend more time going about your life and less time focusing on your dog's every behavior.

After your pup, now dog, exits adolescence there will be regular ups and downs for the next 6-12 months. These ups and downs will be minor, with more ups than downs as your dog is maturing daily, understanding expectations, and

Before You Begin

becoming a natural extension of you and your daily life. With the right dog for the job and the right training throughout, at around 2-3 years of age (depending on personality and breed) your dog will become the reliable Diabetic Alert Dog you were working toward all this time and you will be at an all time "high point" as your dog has become both your best friend and your lifesaver. And the emotional rollercoaster will be worth it time and time again!

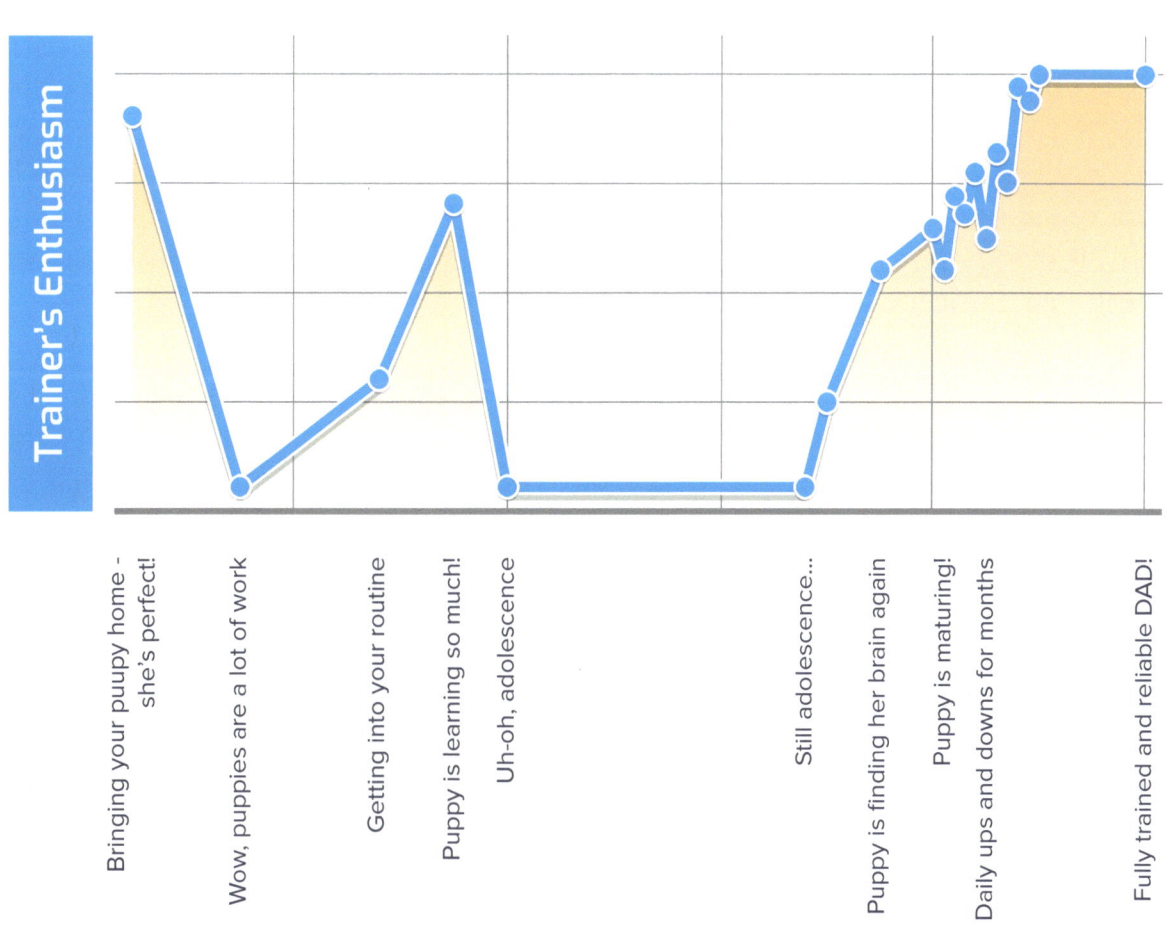

The Emotional Roller Coaster of DAD Training

Before You Begin

Scent Samples

MATERIALS
- ☐ Dental rolls or 2x2 gauze pads
- ☐ Pill bag or graduated vial
- ☐ Glass canning jar

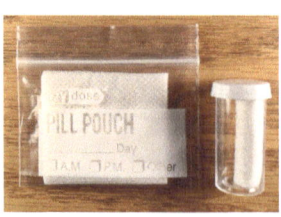

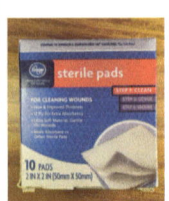

WHAT SAMPLES TO CREATE

Create a saliva sample when your blood sugar is in the range you would like your dog to alert at (e.g. 80mg/dL and below). At first create only low blood sugar samples. Focus on creating samples within 10 mg/dL of the alerting threshold (e.g. If the alerting threshold is 80mg/dL, focus on creating samples between 70-80mg/dL). However, also create lower samples because if a circumstance prohibits your dog from smelling your blood sugar near the alerting threshold, you will still want the dog to alert after it has continued to drop. (By only training levels of 70-80mg/dL, you risk your dog not understanding she should alert to 40mg/dL.) As you progress you will need to create samples when you have high blood sugar and when you are in range as well, to prepare for future training; begin creating these addition samples after you begin Step 10 of the scent training instructions.

WHEN TO CREATE A SAMPLE

Only create a sample if you are able to put the sample in your freezer within 5 minutes of creation and if you are in a safe range. Do not create a sample if there has been any food or drink in your mouth within the past 30 minutes, including gum.

HOW TO CREATE A SAMPLE

STEP 1: When your blood sugar is in a range that you need a sample of, place a dental roll or 2x2 gauze pad directly in your mouth, without touching it (unless you are wearing gloves). You can use the packaging to drop the cotton in your mouth.

STEP 2: Completely saturate the cotton with your saliva, moving it around your mouth.

STEP 3: Without touching the cotton, spit it into a pill baggie or vial, then close

Before You Begin

it tightly.

STEP 4: Use a permanent marker to write the date and glucose at the time of the sample's creation directly on the bag or container.

STEP 5: Place the bag or container into a glass canning jar and screw the lid on tightly before placing it in the freezer.

HOW TO USE SAMPLES

Allow the sample to thaw for a few minutes before presenting it to the dog during a training session. The dogs can smell the sample when frozen, but it is more difficult for them so at the beginning of training let it thaw for 3 minutes.

HOW TO STORE SAMPLES

Always keep the samples in their containers in the freezer unless being used for a training session. After 3 months in the freezer, it is recommended that you discard the samples.

After the training session is completed, place the sample back in its container, (but not in a glass canning jar) and then place it in the fridge. For the next 3 days use the scent sample for training sessions, returning it immediately to the fridge. After 3 days, discard the sample (discard it carefully so your dog cannot smell the sample in the trash).

The most conservative protocol: Discard a sample after 3 months in the freezer, 3 days in the fridge, or 3 hours at room temperature.

The exact length of a sample's lifetime has not been studied. Many have had success keeping samples in other ways that extend the sample's life. Because there is no data proving how long samples can be kept, at the start of training, store according to the most conservative protocol. But once your training is for the purpose of maintaining the alerting skills rather than teaching them, you can experiment with other methods to extend the sample's life. If your experienced DAD does not alert to an old sample, assume that it has expired and discard it. Practice again with a new sample to ensure that the lack of alert was due to the sample's expiration.

 **Before You Begin**

How To Make Scent Tins

Scent tins are the containers that hold the saliva sample while training the dog. This minimizes contamination of the sample and prevents the dog from eating the sample (since the goal is to teach the dog that the sample equals treats, the dog will have a tendency to try to eat the sample ☺)

MATERIALS:
- ☐ (3) ½ ounce metal tins with screw top lid
- ☐ (1) Drill
- ☐ (1) Drill bit

1. Screw a lid onto a metal tin tightly.

2. Drill 5-10 holes into the top of the lid

3. Repeat Steps 1 & 2 for the remaining metal tins. When drilling the holes, either make every pattern random or repeat the exact pattern on each container. This will prevent the dog from associating a certain container with a certain sample.

4. On the bottom of each container, write in permanent marker one of the following: "High" "Low" or "In Range". Be consistent - never change the type of sample that a container holds or your dog will likely become confused due to residual scent.

Before You Begin

How To Build The Scent Wheel

MATERIALS:

- ☐ (1) piece of 18" circular wood
- ☐ (1) Lazy Susan
- ☐ (1) 2" threaded PVC cap
- ☐ (1) 2" PVC snap in drain
- ☐ (8) wood screws
- ☐ (1) Drill
- ☐ (1) Drill bit
- ☐ (1) Permanent marker

18" wood

Threaded PVC cap

Lazy Susan

PVC snap in drain

Cost is approximately $45

1. Place the Lazy Susan approximately in the middle of the 18" wood. Mark the 4 corners where screws will be placed. Remove the Lazy Susan and drill holes where you marked the 4 corners.

2. Place the Lazy Susan back onto the wood, aligning the 4 corners with the drilled holes. Screw the Lazy Susan to the wood.

3. Flip the wood over. Mark 4 locations to form the shape of a square (this is where containers will be placed). Each of the 4 locations should be 2 inches from the outside edge.

4. Drill a hole in one of the 4 marked locations, halfway through the piece of wood. Also drill a hole through the approximate center of a PVC cap.

5. Align the hold in the PVC cap on top of one of the 4 holes drilled into the wood; screw the PVC cap into the wood.

6. Repeat Steps 4 & 5 for the remaining 3 marked locations on the wood.

7. Place the snap in drains in each PVC cap.

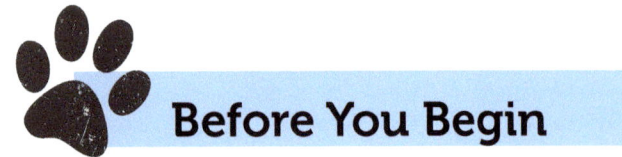
Before You Begin

Daily Training Schedule

The following pages show an example training schedule for the first month of raising a DAD; this schedule was implemented with an 8 week old puppy, beginning the day I brought her home.

This should give you an idea of what my puppies' first month looks like. Some of the activities and experiences were specific to my schedule at the time (e.g. family reunion, road trips, etc.) Don't hesitate to use every part of your life as an opportunity to let your puppy experience new things. This is how she will become a true member of the family and learn to adapt in new environments.

Training sessions should always be kept short and upbeat. Typically I include old commands in a training session to build up a puppy's confidence while also switching to teaching her new behaviors. The schedule provides commands to review, but includes all the commands the pup knows and you do not need to practice every command every training session.

Every interaction you have with your puppy is training, so it is not necessary to have formal training sessions every day. Instead, you can include her training in daily activities such as asking her to "sit stay" before you put her food bowl down, asking her to "watch me" before you open the door, asking her to "down" before you play tug, etc.

With the exception of "Get dressed", all of the obedience commands you should teach your puppy within this first month are explained in the *Puppy Steps* book. (The training schedule in Puppy Steps is similar, but has a few differences because that training schedule is designed for a pet puppy rather than a service dog puppy.)

During the first month of a puppy's life she spends the majority of the day on a leash next to me in the home or in a kennel. This keeps her out of trouble, expedites house training, and helps with bonding. It's important that your puppy has structure in her life to teach her good behaviors. However, it's also crucial that she gets to be a puppy. So when she is on a leash next to me she has toys to play with and is allowed to entertain herself, unless I'm practicing the command "Place".

In the evenings, she almost always gets at least 2 hours of off leash play time outside with our other dogs. This advances her social skills and also lets her have fun and be a puppy. Even after your dog is a fully trained DAD, be sure to let her 'be a dog' at least once a day to keep her happy and let her relax after a hard day's work.

Training - Week 1

Day	Husbandry	Daily Life	Obedience Commands to Review	New Obedience Command(s)	Outings	Scent Training
0	Held her and carried her	Bonding	None	Name Game	None	None
1	Touched paws, teeth, and ears	On a leash beside me all day, except for 2 naps in kennel	Name Game	Crate training, Sit, Down, Stand, Touch	None	None
2	Settle position - touched paws, teeth, and ears	On a leash beside me, 2 naps in kennel	Crate training, Sit, Down, Stand, Touch	Come	Socialization – Lowe's	None
3	None	On a leash beside me, 2 naps in kennel, 30 minute off lead walk on farm	Crate Training, Sit, Down, Stand, Touch, Come	Heel	None	None
4	Settle position - touched paws, teeth, and ears	On a leash beside me, 2 naps in kennel, began learning to play tug	Crate Training, Sit, Down, Stand, Touch, Come, Heel	Watch me, Leave It	Socialization – Farmer's Market	None
5	None	On a leash beside me, extra long (3 hour) nap in kennel, 30 minute off lead walk on farm	Crate Training, Sit, Down, Stand, Touch, Come, Heel, Watch me, Leave It	None	None	None
6	Touched paws, teeth, and ears while tugging	On a leash beside me, 2 naps in kennel, 2 hours free play with other dogs outside	Crate Training, Sit, Down, Stand, Touch, Come, Heel, Watch me, Leave It	None	Socialization – Tractor Supply Co	None
7	None	On a leash beside me, 2 naps in kennel, 1 hour in X-pen outside	Crate Training, Sit, Down, Stand, Touch, Come, Heel, Watch me, Leave It	Sit Stay	None	None

NOTES: _____
_____
_____
_____
_____
_____
_____
_____
_____
_____
_____

Training - Week 2

Day	Husbandry	Daily Life	Obedience Commands to Review	New Obedience Command(s)	Outings	Scent Training
8	Touched belly, ears, and paws while tugging	On a leash beside me, 2 naps in kennel, 30 minute off lead walk, 2 hours free play with other dogs outside	Crate Training, Sit, Down, Stand, Touch, Come, Heel, Watch me, Leave It, Sit Stay	None	Socialization – Home Depot	Step 1, Step 2
9	None	On a leash beside me, 2 naps in kennel, 30 minute off lead walk	Crate Training, Sit, Down, Stand, Touch, Come, Heel, Watch me, Leave It, Sit Stay	Close	None	Step 2
10	Settle position - clipped nails	On a leash beside me, 2 naps in kennel, 2 hours free play with other dogs outside	Crate Training, Sit, Down, Stand, Touch, Come, Heel, Watch me, Leave It, Sit Stay, Close	None	Socialization – Southern States (feed store)	Step 2
11	None	On a leash beside me, 2 naps in kennel, 1 hour in Xpen outside, 2 hours free play with other dogs outside	Crate Training, Sit, Down, Stand, Touch, Come, Heel, Watch me, Leave It, Sit Stay, Close	Down Stay	None	Step 2
12	Settle position – brushed teeth	On a leash beside me, 2 naps in kennel, 2 hours free play with other dogs outside	Crate Training, Sit, Down, Stand, Touch, Come, Heel, Watch me, Leave It, Sit Stay, Close, Down Stay,	Get dressed	None	Step 2, Step 3
13	None	On a leash beside me, 2 naps in kennel, 2 hours free play with other dogs outside	Crate Training, Sit, Down, Stand, Touch, Come, Heel, Watch me, Leave It, Sit Stay, Close, Down Stay, Get Dressed	None	Socialization (practiced public access with vest on, but stayed outside) - Car dealership	Step 2, Step 3
14	None	On a leash beside me, 2 naps in kennel, 2 hours free play with other dogs outside	Crate Training, Sit, Down, Stand, Touch, Come, Heel, Watch me, Leave It, Sit Stay, Close, Down Stay, Get Dressed	None	None	Step 3, Step 4

NOTES: _____
_____
_____
_____
_____
_____
_____
_____
_____
_____

Training - Week 3

Day	Husbandry	Daily Life	Obedience Commands to Review	New Obedience Command(s)	Outings	Scent Training
15	Bath	On a leash beside me, 2 naps in kennel, 2 hours free play with other dogs outside	Crate Training, Sit, Down, Stand, Touch, Come, Heel, Watch me, Leave It, Sit Stay, Down Stay, Close, Get Dressed	Place	Socialization – Family reunion	Step 4, Step 5
16	None	On a leash beside me, 2 naps in kennel, 2 hours free play with other dogs outside	Crate Training, Sit, Down, Stand, Touch, Come, Heel, Watch me, Leave It, Sit Stay, Down Stay, Close, Get Dressed, Place	None	None	Step 4, Step 5
17	Settle position – touched paws, ears, and teeth	On a leash beside me, 2 naps in kennel, 2 hours free play with other dogs outside	Crate Training, Sit, Down, Stand, Touch, Come, Heel, Watch me, Leave It, Sit Stay, Down Stay, Close, Get Dressed, Place (3 minutes)	None	Public Access – Lowe's	Step 5, Step 6
18	None	On a leash beside me, 2 naps in kennel, 2 hours free play with other dogs outside	Crate Training, Sit, Down, Stand, Touch, Come, Heel, Watch me, Leave It, Sit Stay, Down Stay, Close, Get Dressed, Place (5 minutes)	None	None	Step 6
19	Settle position – clipped nails	On a leash beside me, 2 naps in kennel, 2 hours free play with other dogs outside	Crate Training, Sit, Down, Stand, Touch, Come, Heel, Watch me, Leave It, Sit Stay, Down Stay, Close, Get Dressed, Place (10 minutes)	None	Socialization – Outdoor seating at a coffee shop	Step 6
20	None	On a leash beside me, 2 naps in kennel, 2 hours free play with other dogs outside	Crate Training, Sit, Down, Stand, Touch, Come, Heel, Watch me, Leave It, Sit Stay, Down Stay, Close, Get Dressed, Place (15 minutes)	None	None	Step 6
21	None	On a leash beside me, 2 naps in kennel, 2 hours free play with other dogs outside	Crate Training, Sit, Down, Stand, Touch, Come, Heel, Watch me, Leave It, Sit Stay, Down Stay, Close, Get Dressed, Place (20 minutes)	None	None	Step 6, Step 7

NOTES: _____
_____
_____
_____
_____
_____
_____
_____
_____
_____

Training - Week 4

Day	Husbandry	Daily Life	Obedience Commands to Review	New Obedience Command(s)	Outings	Scent Training
22	None	On a leash beside me, 2 naps in kennel, 2 hours free play with other dogs outside	Crate Training, Sit, Down, Stand, Touch, Come, Heel, Watch me, Leave It, Sit Stay, Down Stay, Close, Get Dressed, Place (25 minutes)	None	Public Access – Clothing store	Step 6, Step 7
23	Settle position – brushed teeth	On a leash beside me, 2 naps in kennel, 2 hours free play with other dogs outside	Crate Training, Sit, Down, Stand, Touch, Come, Heel, Watch me, Leave It, Sit Stay, Down Stay, Close, Get Dressed, Place (25 minutes)	None	None	Step 6, Step 8
24	Held in the car	Took a nap in the car during road trip, 2 hours free play with other dogs outside	Crate Training, Sit, Down, Stand, Touch, Come, Heel, Watch me, Leave It, Sit Stay, Down Stay, Close, Get Dressed, Place (30 minutes)	None	Socialization – Road trip	Step 6, Step 8
25	None	On a leash beside me, 2 naps in kennel, 2 hours free play with other dogs outside	Crate Training, Sit, Down, Stand, Touch, Come, Heel, Watch me, Leave It, Sit Stay, Down Stay, Close, Get Dressed, Place (30 minutes)	None	None	Step 6, Step 8
26	Settle position – clipped nails	On a leash beside me, 2 naps in kennel, 2 hours free play with other dogs outside	Crate Training, Sit, Down, Stand, Touch, Come, Heel, Watch me, Leave It, Sit Stay, Down Stay, Close, Get Dressed, Place (35 minutes)	None	Public Access – Grocery Store (Kroger)	Step 6, Step 8
27	None	On a leash beside me, 2 naps in kennel, 2 hours free play with other dogs outside	Crate Training, Sit, Down, Stand, Touch, Come, Heel, Watch me, Leave It, Sit Stay, Down Stay, Close, Get Dressed, Place (35 minutes)	None	None	Step 6, Step 8
28	None		Crate Training, Sit, Down, Stand, Touch, Come, Heel, Watch me, Leave It, Sit Stay, Down Stay, Close, Get Dressed, Place (40 minutes)	None	None	Step 6, Step 8

NOTES: _____
_____
_____
_____
_____
_____
_____
_____
_____
_____

M.D. Dogs Inc
Diabetic Alert Dog Training Steps

Choosing Your Dog

Choosing Your Dog

A Flowchart For Choosing A Dog

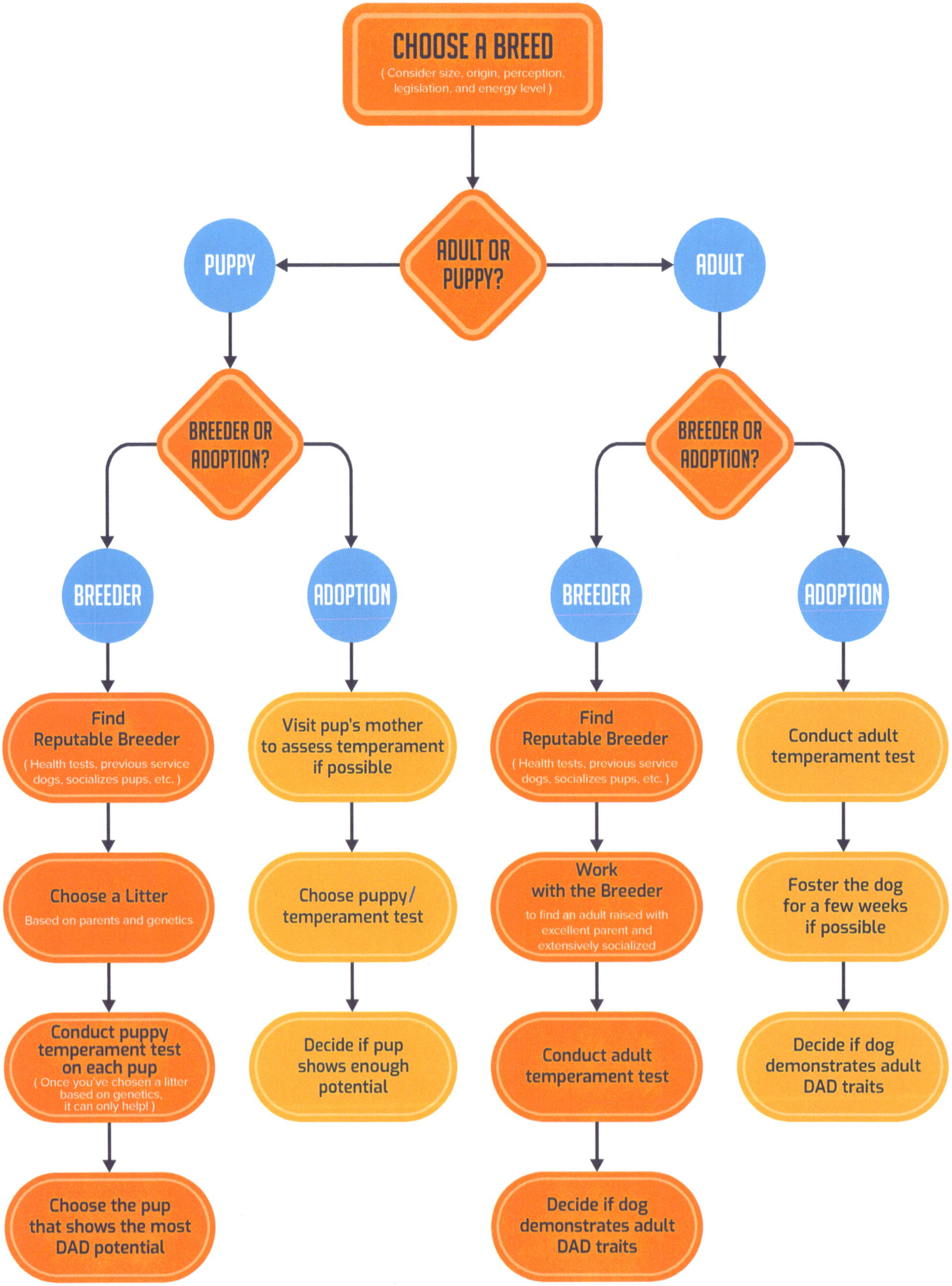

CHOOSE A BREED
(Consider size, origin, perception, legislation, and energy level)

↓

ADULT OR PUPPY?

PUPPY

BREEDER OR ADOPTION?

BREEDER
- **Find Reputable Breeder** (Health tests, previous service dogs, socializes pups, etc.)
- **Choose a Litter** — Based on parents and genetics
- **Conduct puppy temperament test on each pup** (Once you've chosen a litter based on genetics, it can only help!)
- **Choose the pup that shows the most DAD potential**

ADOPTION
- Visit pup's mother to assess temperament if possible
- Choose puppy/temperament test
- Decide if pup shows enough potential

ADULT

BREEDER OR ADOPTION?

BREEDER
- **Find Reputable Breeder** (Health tests, previous service dogs, socializes pups, etc.)
- **Work with the Breeder** to find an adult raised with excellent parent and extensively socialized
- **Conduct adult temperament test**
- **Decide if dog demonstrates adult DAD traits**

ADOPTION
- Conduct adult temperament test
- Foster the dog for a few weeks if possible
- Decide if dog demonstrates adult DAD traits

Choosing Your Dog

When choosing your dog, there are many things to keep in mind. In the following pages I address topics to think about when choosing your DAD and further explain the suggestions outlined in the flowchart. These are just guidelines. If you already have a dog at home that you are hoping to train as a DAD, you can still try to train that dog, even if it's not a recommended breed! Just read through the below guidelines to know what to be aware of and what to expect. This is primarily written for those picking out a dog specifically for a DAD in order to set them up for success.

Genetics: The most accurate prediction of whether a puppy will be capable of being a service dog is the puppy's genetics. Genetics hardwire a dog to have certain traits and tendencies; so when looking for a puppy to become a service dog, make sure to meet both parents and test them. Would each parent make a good service dog? The parents don't have to be well trained - behaviors such as jumping up, bouncing, and exuberance are just matters of training. But when you meet the parents focus on behaviours such as vocalization, confidence, wariness, and guarding - these tend to be highly heritable traits that you want to avoid. Look for parents that are confident, quiet, friendly, enthusiastic, and food motivated in addition to having all health clearances, as these are positive traits that will likely be passed onto the puppies.

Genetics provide the foundation which determines if a dog has the potential to ever become a service dog, and the raising and training of the dog either assists that potential, or eliminates it.

Size of breed: If your dog is only for a DAD, there is no reason to choose a huge breed. Large breeds are inconvenient in public and it is hard for them to be inconspicuous. But having a tiny breed can be difficult as well, as they are at risk of being stepped on, and it is harder to notice their alerts or for them to retrieve items. 20 to 60 pound dogs tend to be the most common and convenient size.

Origin of breed: Know the origin of your breed so you know their weaknesses. Terriers usually have a tendency to be independent, dig, and bark because they were bred to hunt vermin. Herding breeds have a tendency to chase children or animals in an attempt to herd, so it may be difficult in a house of active, small children. Sporting breeds, especially retrievers, are going to have a tendency to chase balls or

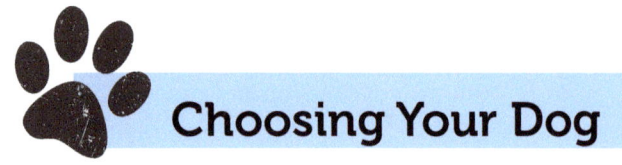

Choosing Your Dog

birds and have high prey drive, so it may be hard to teach them to ignore squirrels or birds and may not be the right choice if you are a tennis player. While many think a hound would be a good choice because of their superb scenting abilities, they are actually one of the most difficult because they are obsessive about using their noses in the environment around them and it is difficult to keep their attention. Typically sporting breeds are the most common for DAD training, with herding breeds being the second most popular.

Perception of breed: While you can absolutely use a bully breed, Rottweiler, or similar dog as a DAD, this is going to make your life more difficult. More people will fear your dog and cause a scene, and you are more likely to have access issues. However, extremely small breeds such as Chihuahuas and Dachshunds are likely to result in more access issues as well because so many dogs of those breeds are falsely represented as service dogs. If you already have one of these breeds you still can train them to be a DAD. But if you are searching for a breed to train, I recommend avoiding large, intimidating breeds as well as especially small breeds to avoid making public access more difficult for yourself.

Laws: Some locations have breed restrictions. While your service dog is typically exempt from breed restriction laws (in the U.S.), certain breeds cause a landlord's insurance fees to increase. If a landlord's insurance will increase as a result of your breed of service dog, the landlord is not required to allow you to live on his or her property. If you do not own your own home and land, or there is any chance you will need to rent a home, I would not recommend using a breed that might be on a breed restriction list.

Energy level: Choose a breed that will match your activity level. If you are out and about working all day, attending meetings, exercising, and going to social events, you will want a dog that can keep up with you. But if you work from home and do not run regularly, or attend school and do not plan on bringing the dog with you, then you will need a lower energy dog

Choosing Your Dog

that can cope with that lifestyle. For example, do not choose a Border Collie if you are not extremely active; similarly it would not be best to choose a Newfoundland if you are always on the go.

Brachycephalic (short nosed) breeds: Originally it was believed that these breeds (Pug, Shih Tzu, Chihuahua, Chow Chow, Pekingese, Lhasa Apso, Bull Mastiff, and English Toy Spaniel) should not be used because their scent detection capabilities are inferior to other breeds. However, this has not been scientifically proven. With that being said, these breeds are not recommended for other reasons – they have airways that are more susceptible to damage and they struggle with breathing if they are exercising or in hot and humid weather. Because a DAD is supposed to help keep you safe, your DAD needs to be physically able to accompany you in as many situations as possible which these breeds cannot do.

Coat type: Coat type is typically the least important factor to consider, however if you are choosing a breed specifically to be a DAD it is best to think about this before deciding. It is much easier to keep a short haired dog clean and well groomed than dealing with a thick coated or long haired breed. Additionally, choosing a dog that does not shed much would be beneficial if the DAD will ever be attending work or school because this will minimize the effect on those who are allergic.

Breed recommendations: Typically, the breeds Golden Retrievers, Labrador Retrievers, Poodles, and mixes thereof are used as DADs. Organizations have researched and found that these breeds are most successful, so they are strongly recommended.

Breeder or Rescue: DADs are meant to keep you healthy and safe. Because of this, I choose to take the fewest number of risks possible and this means purchasing a dog from a reputable breeder. The first reason for this is that the dog will most likely be healthier - while there are still no guarantees, as even reputable breeders sometimes have dogs with health problems, it will minimize the risk. It will also help significantly reduce the chance of getting a puppy that has a life threatening disease such as Parvo.

What is a reputable breeder: A reputable breeder performs health testing on the parent dogs to ensure the puppies being born will be as

Choosing Your Dog

healthy as possible. These health tests should include checking the dogs' joints for hip dysplasia and/or elbow dysplasia, checking their eyes, and any breed specific testing. Ask for proof of these health clearances (In the United States, health screenings for hips and elbows will usually be certifications from PennHIP or OFA.)

Additionally, you should be able to visit the facilities and ensure the puppies are in a clean environment and receiving age appropriate socialization experiences.

The puppies should be kept at the breeder's facility with their siblings until 8 weeks of age. If puppies are released prior to this age they will not receive the necessary socialization experiences they need; remaining with their siblings teaches the puppies behaviors such as how to play appropriately, bite inhibition, and how to recover.

Ask the breeder if you can see the mother. Ensure the mother of the puppies is friendly, with a good temperament and is well taken care of. Also be sure that the breeder truly cares for the dogs and knows them personally. If the breeder does not know the puppies then most likely they are not interacting with them so they are not getting the human interaction needed to develop into stable adults.

A reputable breeder will typically require you to sign a contract that indicates if you do not care for the puppy or are unable to keep it, you will return the dog to the breeder.

The price range of puppies varies greatly. Do not choose a dog because it is the cheapest. Additionally, the most expensive dog is not necessarily coming from the best breeder. Do your research and make sure your dog is coming from a good environment that will set you up for success.

Choosing Your Dog

Ideal Puppy Traits

While genetics are the most important factor, once you choose a litter based on the parents and are deciding between littermates, a temperament test and general observations can help differentiate between puppies.

When I evaluate puppies I perform temperament tests (next page) on each one and analyze the puppies' responses and scores objectively. However, during the test and apart from the test I also look for specific personality traits that are suited to becoming a Diabetic Alert Dog (traits listed below). Ask an experienced service dog trainer to accompany you to help identify which ones demonstrate these traits and would likely enjoy becoming a Diabetic Alert Dog.

Confident: She does not get scared frequently.

Curious: She investigates new things. She can be hesitant but she has a drive to explore and learn more about objects, sounds, and people.

Food motivated: She is excited to eat low value rewards such as kibble.

Persistent: She will continue working for a piece of low value treat even if she doesn't succeed at first.

Active: She runs and plays frequently. It's important to look at the puppies multiple times because puppies do sleep a lot so if you happen to see a puppy being particularly calm, that does not mean it is not a good candidate. But if you visit a few times and the same puppy is always exceptionally calm, then that is not a good candidate. However, you don't want a hyperactive puppy either, so be careful to avoid the extremes.

People focused: She is excited to visit with new people and does not show hesitancy to interact.

Forgiving: If you restrain her she returns to you, licks your face, or rolls over, rather than leaving you or refusing to interact.

Quick to recover: If she is frightened by something she may startle but within a few seconds returns to it to investigate it further.

Social: She interacts with people but also interacts with other puppies. If she has no interest in the other dogs she may have poor canine social skills or develop separation anxiety.

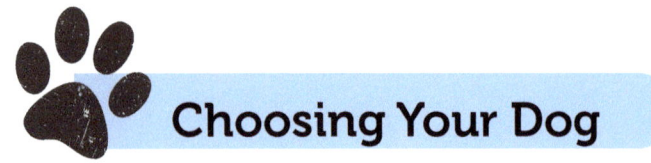

Choosing Your Dog

Puppy Temperament Test

The goal for this test is to help you choose the best candidate for a Diabetic Alert Dog. The test is designed for puppies that are 49 days old and still living with their siblings. It should be performed in an area the puppies have not experienced before and during the test the puppy should not be within sight of its siblings.

As puppies mature, many factors affect how they respond and grow. Because of this, we can never definitively know what a puppy's adult temperament will be. However, this test is designed to predict it as best we can. This test is designed to demonstrate each puppy's strengths and weaknesses. No puppy is the perfect DAD candidate, so this test won't necessarily show you exactly which puppy to choose. Instead, the goal is to allow you to see which puppies have which weaknesses and what environment the puppy would succeed in. This allows you to make an educated decision about which puppy is right for you.

There is not a 'correct score' for each exercise. The score you will want for your candidate on each test will depend on the environment she will be in. In general, lower scores are best for more active environments while higher scores are best if a calm dog is needed. Avoid puppies that score 1's or 5's as those are extreme responses that are rarely demonstrated by a suitable DAD candidate.

It is best if a local service dog trainer is able to test the puppies for you, or accompany you while you test them. This will allow you to make a decision based on the opinion of a professional who has experience with canine body language and behavior.

One thing to keep in mind is to not choose a puppy because it chose you. Be as objective as possible when performing these tests in order to assess the puppies equally. If there is a puppy that is extremely attached to you, while adorable and heartwarming, it could mean the puppy is insecure or will have separation anxiety in the future so avoid that puppy. Similarly, if there is a puppy that does not want anything to do with you, do not choose that puppy either.

In general, choose a puppy that is happy to interact with you, but also happy to interact with her siblings and curious about her environment. And remember, genetics are a more accurate prediction. So if choosing between a litter with parents known to have an excellent temperament, or a puppy who scored well on a temperament test but no parental information, choose the puppy with known excellent parents for a greater chance of success.

COPY THE FOLLOWING PAGES FOR AS MANY PUPPIES AS YOU WILL BE TESTING SO THAT EACH PUPPY HAS THEIR OWN TEMPERAMENT TEST DOCUMENTATION.

The MD Dogs' Puppy Temperament Test is based upon the Volhard Puppy Aptitude Test by Wendy Volhard, with modifications to reflect traits needed for successful Diabetic Alert Dogs using MD Dogs training methods. To learn more about the Volhard Puppy Aptitude test please visit: https://www.volharddognutrition.com/choosing-your-puppy-pat/

Puppy Name:
_____

Choosing Your Dog

Temperament Test Exercises

1. **APPROACHING STRANGER** Tester places the puppy on the ground and walks approximately 3 feet away, then turns to encourage the puppy to come to them. Tester can kneel or bend over and talk to puppy or clap hands.

   1. Came quickly, enthusiastically, jumped at hands, and bit hands
   2. Came quickly, enthusiastically jumped and/or licked at hands
   3. Came readily
   4. Came hesitantly
   5. Didn't come

   NOTES:_____
   _____
   _____
   _____

2. **FOLLOWING** Directly after Test 1, tester turns around and walks away from puppy slowly, encouraging the puppy to follow by talking to the puppy in a happy tone. (Make sure the puppy sees you walk away).

   1. Followed quickly, tail up, got underfoot, bit at feet
   2. Followed readily, tail up, got underfoot
   3. Followed readily
   4. Followed hesitantly
   5. Didn't follow

   NOTES:_____
   _____
   _____
   _____

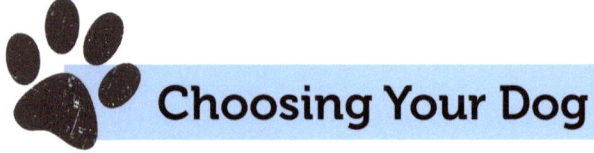

Choosing Your Dog

3. **RESTRAINT** Tester kneels down and gently places the puppy on its back and holds it on its back for 30 seconds. Hold the puppy with as little pressure as possible, while still keeping it on its back.

1. Struggled fiercely, flailed, used mouth
2. Struggled fiercely, flailed
3. Both struggled and settled
4. Did not struggle
5. Did not struggle, strained to avoid eye contact

NOTES:_____
_____
_____
_____

4. **FORGIVENESS** Immediately after Test 3, tester allows puppy to get up then gently strokes it from head to back while tester is still kneeling. Have puppy at the side of tester and tester's face low enough for puppy to reach if it desires, but not hovering over puppy.

1. Left tester to enthusiastically explore, play, etc.
2. Jumped to reach tester's face
3. Stayed by tester and squirmed, rolled over, or licked hands
4. Stayed by tester, but did not interact
5. Went away and stayed away calmly

NOTES:_____
_____
_____
_____

32 M.D. Dogs Inc. Training Your Pet To Be Your Partner

Choosing Your Dog

5. **ELEVATION** Tester supports the puppy's chest and belly while holding all four feet a few inches above the ground. Tester keeps puppy elevated for 30 seconds.

   1. Struggled fiercely, flailed, used mouth

   2. Struggled fiercely, flailed

   3. Both struggled and settled

   4. Did not struggle, relaxed

   5. Did not struggle, stiff

   NOTES:_____
   _____
   _____
   _____

6. **RETRIEVAL** Tester kneels beside puppy and gets it interested in a crumpled piece of paper. When puppy shows interest, tester gently tosses it 1-3 feet in front of the puppy. If puppy doesn't see it, repeat up to 2 times.

   1. Chased object, picked it up and ran away

   2. Chased object, reached it, then did not pick it up or return

   3. Chased object, returned to tester with object (within a few feet of tester)

   4. Chased object and returned to tester without object

   5. Did not chase object

   NOTES:_____
   _____
   _____
   _____

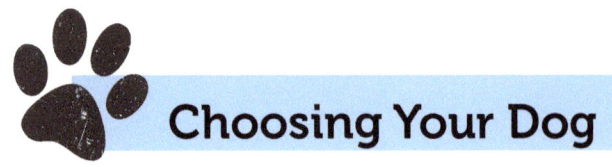

Choosing Your Dog

7. **PHYSICAL SENSITIVITY** Tester lightly squeezes the webbing of the puppy's front paw, between two of its toes. Tester gradually increases pressure while counting to ten. As soon as puppy pulls away, tester stops.

   1. 9-10 count before pulling away
   2. 7-8 count before pulling away
   3. 5-6 count before pulling away
   4. 3-4 count before pulling away
   5. 1-2 count before pulling away

   NOTES:_____
   _____
   _____

8. **SOUND SENSITIVITY** The puppy is placed in the center of the testing area and a few feet away tester makes a sharp noise. Tester can continue to make noise to determine puppy's response.

   1. Located sound and barked at it
   2. Located sound and ran towards it
   3. Located sound and walked toward it showing curiosity or ignored it
   4. Backed away from sound and avoided area
   5. Cringed

   NOTES:_____
   _____
   _____
   _____

Choosing Your Dog

9. **TOY DRIVE** Tester ties a leash to a bath towel. Tester places puppy in the center of the testing area and places it on the ground, then jerks it across the ground approximately 2-3 feet away from the puppy.

1. Attacked object, bit it, and tugged
2. Put feet and mouth on object
3. Looked with curiosity and attempted to investigate
4. Observed with tail down
5. Avoided object, backed away from it, or hid

NOTES:_____
_____
_____

10. **VISUAL SENSITIVITY** The tester opens an umbrella 3-5 feet from the puppy, then gently places it on the ground.

1. Ran to umbrella and bit it or barked at it
2. Enthusiastically went towards umbrella
3. Walked to umbrella to investigate it
4. Watched but did not move towards umbrella
5. Avoided umbrella, backed away, or hid from it

NOTES:_____
_____
_____

Choosing Your Dog

11. **SCENT DETECTION** A large piece of meat is placed on the ground with a milk crate or similar barrier placed over top to prevent access. The tester then places the puppy 3-5 feet away from the meat and waits next to the meat to see if the puppy finds it. If the puppy does not find it after 30 seconds or so, tester can encourage puppy by walking around the meat or calling the puppy away from distractions, towards the meat. If after another 30 seconds the puppy still has not found it, tester can tap the milk crate or barrier to assist the puppy.

1. Located scent (with or without any assistance), but was not interested

2. Located scent when tester walked around the barrier and/or called puppy to assist

3. Located scent independently in less than 30 seconds, and showed interest.

4. Located scent after tester tapped the barrier to assist.

5. Did not locate scent even with assistance from tester

NOTES:_____
_____
_____
_____

Choosing Your Dog

12. **SCENT PERSISTENCE** The tester places the puppy in front of a simple dog puzzle or slow feeder with 3 pieces of meat inside. If the puppy doesn't notice the puzzle or slow feeder, the tester may encourage the puppy to interact by tapping it and verbally encouraging.

  1. Bit or barked at the puzzle (demonstrating frustration)
  2. Persisted for >10 seconds using one technique to reach the food
  3. Persisted for >10 seconds using multiple techniques (mouthing, pawing, etc.)
  4. Persisted for 1-10 seconds before losing interest
  5. Did not persist

  NOTES:_____
  _____
  _____
  _____

13. **BIDDABILITY** The tester has 3 low value treats (e.g. pieces of dog food). With the puppy in front of the tester, the tester lets the puppy eat one treat. Then the tester places another low value treat between his or her forefinger and thumb and moves the treat in large circles or figure 8's to see if the puppy follows, then gives the puppy the treat. With the third treat, the tester lures the puppy into a sit.

  1. Frequently bit at lure or tester's hand
  2. Continuously followed the lure – difficult to lure into "Sit"
  3. Continuously followed the lure – easy to lure into "Sit"
  4. Attempted to follow lure, but lost interest in treat
  5. Did not attempt to follow lure

  NOTES:_____
  _____
  _____
  _____

Choosing Your Dog

PUPPY SCORE SUMMARY

1. _____   4. _____   7. _____   10. _____   13. _____

2. _____   5. _____   8. _____   11. _____

3. _____   6. _____   9. _____   12. _____

PUPPY TEMPERAMENT SUMMARY

Strengths: _____   Weaknesses: _____

_____   _____

_____   _____

_____   _____

_____   _____

_____   _____

_____   _____

_____   _____

Choosing Your Dog

Choosing an Adult Dog

If you are choosing an adult dog to train as a DAD, look for the correct personality rather than focusing on the minor details. Do not choose a dog because it already knows commands such as sit, down, or shake. While it's great that you won't have to train those commands, these types of commands are very simple and take only a few days to teach. You will be teaching the dog so much over the next year that having to teach these simple behaviors should not be a factor.

Instead, look for broader personality traits that indicate the dog is stable, confident, will learn easily, and will enjoy being a service dog.

If possible, it is best to have the dog for a trial period because adult dogs often act differently based on their environment. Especially if you are choosing a dog from a rescue or shelter, you will want to remove the dog from the environment for a few days if possible because being in a kennel surrounded by other dogs with little human interaction will result in different behaviors than when in a home. Typically it takes 2 weeks in a home for a dog to show their true temperament, so a few days trial period will not show the entire personality, but it will still be an improvement from evaluating in the rescue or shelter setting. The ideal situation is to foster the dog for at least 2 weeks.

Finding an adult service dog candidate is a difficult task. Many dogs are surrendered because of behavioral or physical problems. Do not go to a shelter or rescue with the intent to choose a dog immediately. You may need to visit 10 or more locations before finding the right candidate. Be picky and continue searching until you find one that has potential and will set you up for success. Additionally, be sure that it is completely healthy and has not had any medical conditions. Even then, there is still a large risk in that you do not know the health of the parents or any information about the dog's history.

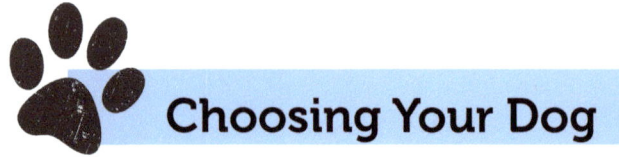

Choosing Your Dog

Ideal Adult Dog Traits

- **Confidence** – Tail up, tall stance, dog is relaxed when exploring.

- **Curiosity** – Interested in exploring and investigating, does not avoid or shy away from new situations or objects.

- **Food motivation** – Ideally is willing to work for low value rewards such as kibble, or medium value rewards such as Zuke's Mini Naturals.

- **Friendliness** – happy to greet people and be pet without shying away.

- **Quick recovery** – When startled, dog recovers quickly and continues acting normally without trembling, showing any aggression, or becoming nervous.

- **Tolerance** – When experiencing slight discomfort dog does not show aggression, become fearful, or jump away (shying away slightly is reasonable).

- **No dog aggression** – When a strange dog is near by, dog is relaxed and ignores dog or is curious.

- **No resource guarding** – When dog has a high value toy or food, it does not demonstrate any aggression or possessiveness when approached by a person or dog.

- **No handling sensitivity** – Dog is calm and relaxed while its ears, teeth, eyes, paws, belly, and tail are examined and held for a few seconds each.

- **Persistence** – Willing to work for treats and continues to attempt multiple times without giving up.

Scent Training

M.D. Dogs Inc
Diabetic Alert Dog Training Steps
Scent Training Steps

Scent Training

Step 1
Beginning to pair the reward with the scent

Instructions:
Place a low scent sample in the scent tin that has holes in the top. Present the tin in front of the dog – a few inches from her nose. When she investigates it, immediately mark and reward. **Repeat approximately 20 times.**

TIPS

- Reward the dog at the scent source. Hold the reward at the top of the container, on the holes, so the dog associates the scent with the reward.

- Use high value rewards – meat or cheese work great!

Scent Training

Step # __1__

Location(s): _____

Training Date(s): _____

Time(s) Spent: _____

NOTES: _____

_____

_____

_____

_____

_____

_____

_____

_____

_____

_____

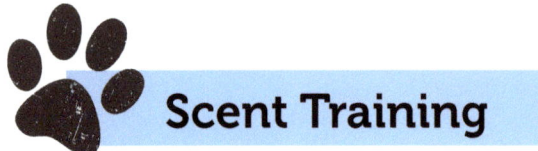

Scent Training

Step 2
Sniffing the sample

Instructions:

Present the scent tin in front of the dog and wait for her to actually sniff it, then mark and reward. **Repeat approximately 100 times.**

TIPS

- You know she is sniffing when you see her nostrils flare or you hear her inhale or exhale, while her nose is touching or almost touching the container.

- If after 5 different sessions your dog still isn't sniffing, put a piece of kibble in the scent tin along with the sample to encourage sniffing. The sample will then need to be thrown out after each session that a kibble is added, but try this for a few repetitions, being sure to mark and reward for sniffing. Then repeat this step but with a sample in a brand new scent tin (without any kibble contamination), and mark and reward for the dog sniffing despite no traces of kibble. Fade out the kibble as quickly as possible to avoid teaching your dog to alert to kibble!

- Always end a training session positively and after a success.

Scent Training

Step # __2__

Location(s): _____

Training Date(s): _____

Time(s) Spent: _____

NOTES: _____

_____

_____

_____

_____

_____

_____

_____

_____

_____

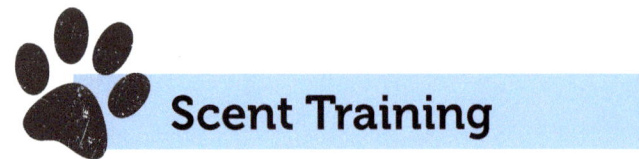

Scent Training

Step 3
Pawing the sample

Instructions:

Repeat Step 2, but withhold the reward until the dog attempts to use her paw. As soon as she makes any movement with her paw (even if she doesn't make contact with the tin), mark and reward. Throughout the repetitions, begin to raise the criteria so she is only rewarded for making contact with the tin. **Repeat approximately 50 times.**

TIPS

- Some puppies will use their paw before you intend - reward it!

- Be patient and don't cue your dog to use her paw - we want them to be independent.

- If she doesn't try to use her paw even when you wait for 30 seconds on 3 attempts, lower the container closer to her paw. If she lifts her paw at all, mark and reward! Then only reward when she paws the container. After 20 repetitions raise the container higher. If she never lifts her paw, return to Step 2 to create more value for the container.

Scent Training

Step # __3__

Location(s): _____

Training Date(s): _____

Time(s) Spent: _____

NOTES: _____

_____

_____

_____

_____

_____

_____

_____

_____

_____

_____

Scent Training

Step 4
Pawing a hidden sample

Instructions:
Repeat Step 3 but enclose the container in your hand. **Repeat approximately 30 times.**

TIPS

- The purpose of this is to teach the dog early on that the scent can occur without the metal tins – we want to avoid teaching them to rely on the visual cue.

- If you have used a larger tin in the past, you may need to buy a small one, such as a ½ oz or 1 oz tin, so that you can fit it entirely in your hand.

- You can also practice proofing your dog off of the container by switching containers – tea infusers work well! *Repeat with each new container at least 50 times.*

Scent Training

Step # __4__ :

Location(s): _____

Training Date(s): _____

Time(s) Spent: _____

NOTES: _____

_____

_____

_____

_____

_____

_____

_____

_____

_____

Scent Training

Step 5
Pawing at different positions

Instructions:

With a low sample inside the scent tin, close your hand around the tin and hold it at different positions – at your side, on the ground, behind you, and above their head. Mark and reward each time she paws your hand. ***Repeat approximately 40 times.***

TIPS

- After the dog is confident, gradually encourage persistence by waiting just a little longer before rewarding. The goal is to teach the dog to keep pawing until they are rewarded, which helps in the future if you are not responding to an alert.

Scent Training

Step # __5__

Location(s): _____

Training Date(s): _____

Time(s) Spent: _____

NOTES: _____

_____

_____

_____

_____

_____

_____

_____

_____

_____

_____

Step 6
Checking critical locations

Instructions:

With a low sample inside the scent tin, practice having your dog alert to it while you hold it at your left ankle, left knee, right knee, then right ankle. Perform 2-5 repetitions in each location before moving to the next location. Reward each time she sniffs and paws it.

Repeat this whole routine 200 times.

TIPS

- The scent of low blood sugar is strong at your knees and feet, so this step teaches the dog to check these locations for the scent. The dog will then begin to check these places on their own to determine if they should alert.

- Do the same pattern each time so that your dog learns to 'check you'.

- Practice this step in numerous locations to teach the dog to always be checking you (home, pet store, parking lot, etc.)

- After about 50 repetitions of this step, you can start Step 7. But continue to practice this step even after you move on to the next few steps to reach at least 200 total repetitions.

Scent Training

Step # __6__

Location(s): _____

Training Date(s): _____

Time(s) Spent: _____

NOTES: _____

_____

_____

_____

_____

_____

_____

_____

_____

_____

Scent Training

Step 7
Eliminating the scent tin

Instructions:

Hold a low scent sample in your hand without a container, then present your hand in front of the dog. When the dog sniffs and paws your hand, mark and reward excitedly.
Repeat approximately 20 times.

TIPS

- Wash your hands before and after handling the scent sample to minimize contamination.

- For this step, after you have used a sample once, do not use it again because it will be contaminated from being in your hand; the sample will now include traces of other odors such as the last soap you used to wash your hands and the last food you touched.

Scent Training

Step # __7__

Location(s): _____

Training Date(s): _____

Time(s) Spent: _____

NOTES: _____

_____

_____

_____

_____

_____

_____

_____

_____

_____

Scent Training

Step 8
Pawing a person

Instructions:

Part A) While standing, hold a low scent sample in your fist, against your legs. When the dog sniffs and paws your fist or leg, mark and reward excitedly.

Repeat approximately 20 times.

Part B) While standing, let her sniff the sample, then move it a few inches higher as she is trying to paw it so that she misses the sample and paws your leg. Reward her for attempting to paw your leg without jumping up. You can reward her for pawing the air or pawing your leg, just not jumping up.

Repeat approximately 50 times.

TIPS

- This helps teach the dog the mechanics of how to paw your leg.

- Wash your hands before and after handling the scent sample.

- After you have used a sample once during this step, do not use it again because it will be contaminated from being in your hand.

Scent Training

Step # __8__

Location(s): _____

Training Date(s): _____

Time(s) Spent: _____

NOTES: _____

_____

_____

_____

_____

_____

_____

_____

_____

_____

_____

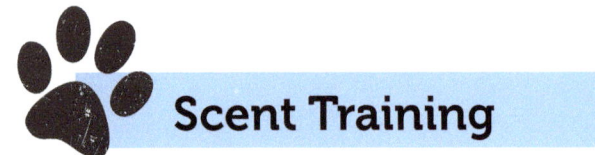

Scent Training

Step 9
Alerting based on scent alone

Instructions:

With the dog out of sight, rub the scent sample on your foot, hand, or back of knee. Casually be near your dog while acting natural. Wait for her to detect the scent and paw you. When she does, have a "Puppy Party" - give her 3 or 4 high value treats and lots of praise. After about 2 minutes of treats and praise, you can give a phrase "All better".

Repeat 4-5 times each week for the rest of your dog's working life.

TIPS

- Do not give body language cues! Don't stare at her or blow on her, just be patient and wait. Otherwise she will rely on those additional cues before alerting.

- If the first few times she sniffs in the general area, but hesitates to alert, you can gently encourage her by asking "What is it?". But fade that out within the first 5-6 times.

- Put the scent sample away after rubbing it on yourself, before going near her. After the alerting and party, wash off the saliva from the area you rubbed it on and anything else that it touched.

- If you have long pants and shoes on and cannot rub the sample on your skin, then put the scent sample in one of your metal tins and hide it in one of those locations – foot, hand, or knee. You can put it in your sock, your rolled up pant leg, top of your shoe, etc.

- Practice frequently in every situation possible. In the Records section of this book there is a scent training checklist with suggested training locations to prepare your dog to confidently live alert no matter the environment.

- Always have materials to clean the area after she alerts and has been rewarded - otherwise you are teaching her to ignore the scent. If you are going to practice in public, be sure to have access to a bathroom so you can clean the area with soap and water, or bring disinfectant wipes.

Scent Training

Step # __9__

Location(s): _____

Training Date(s): _____

Time(s) Spent: _____

NOTES: _____

_____

_____

_____

_____

_____

_____

_____

_____

_____

_____

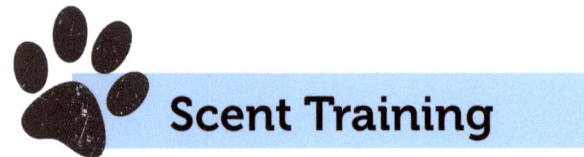

Scent Training

Step 10
Solidifying the dog's understanding

Instructions:

Part A) Present two identical scent tins in front of the dog – one with a low scent sample and one empty. The low should be closest to the dog. When she sniffs the one with the low sample, immediately mark and reward excitedly! (Do not wait for a paw behavior, reward for just a sniff in all parts of this step.) *Only 1 repetition.*

Part B) Switch the scent tins behind your back so they are in different locations when you present them to the dog again – now the low should be furthest from her. When she sniffs the correct tin, mark and reward. *Only 1 repetition.*

Part C) Switch them behind your back again. Mark and reward when she sniffs the correct one. *Only 1 repetition. (Repeat the entire step a maximum of 3 times/session)*

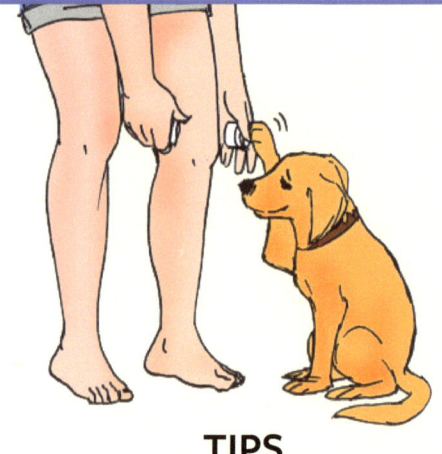

TIPS

- If she paws the incorrect container, freeze and wait for her to just sniff the correct one.

- Many dogs fail Part B, sniffing and pawing the incorrect tin. Just wait for her to sniff the correct one and then move on to Part C.

- This exercise solidifies your dog's understanding that the smell of low blood sugar results in rewards, and helps to prevent the dog from solely focusing on the final behavior of pawing. If the dog is rewarded too much for the paw behavior and the scent is not reinforced along the way, the dog will likely begin to haphazardly paw anything you present to her.

- This step can be practiced for just 1 session and does not need to be practiced throughout your dog's working life. This is only used to demonstrate in these early stages of training that the scent is most important and to prevent overemphasizing the paw behavior. If at any point your dog begins to paw without sniffing, return to this step for a few sessions.

Scent Training

Step # __10__

Location(s): _____

Training Date(s): _____

Time(s) Spent: _____

NOTES: _____

_____
_____
_____
_____
_____
_____
_____
_____
_____
_____

Scent Training

Step 11
Teaching the scent wheel

Instructions:

Part A) Place a low sample in a scent tin and put it in a scent wheel compartment. Place blank (empty) scent tins in the remaining compartments. Walk backwards around the wheel with your dog in front of you. Use your hand to encourage her to sniff each compartment. Continue walking, don't force her to sniff every container. When she hesitates/sits/paws at the container with the low, mark and reward. Then spin the wheel and repeat. Gradually raise the criteria so you only reward when she sits and paws the container.

Repeat approximately 100 times.

Part B) When she is succeeding 95% of the time, repeat Part A but place dry cotton in the blank scent tins instead of leaving them empty.

Part C) When she is succeeding 95% of the time, repeat Part A but place in range saliva samples (non alerting levels of blood sugar) in the scent tins instead of leaving them empty. Vary the in range samples over many training sessions to teach her to ignore everything except what you want her to alert to.

Repeat at least 50 times over multiple days, but it is beneficial to practice throughout your dog's working life.

Scent Training

TIPS

- The first few times, begin having her check the container that has the sample in it first. This will teach her that there is a low in this new contraption and when she finds it she gets rewarded. Then gradually start further away from the positive sample, so she has to check empty containers before finding the low.

- Use a leash to gently guide her so she doesn't walk on the wheel. In the beginning, if she walks on the wheel and finds the correct container, still reward her. But use her reward to lure her into the correct position (in front of the correct container) before giving it to her. It can also help to place the wheel on a box so it's a little taller.

- At first it will be a little messy, but be gentle and patient - as you practice she will begin to understand that she should walk around the wheel and sniff each container until she finds one to alert to.

- While you spin the wheel, hold her away from the wheel, then release her to go check again. This 'resets' her. You can let her nibble on a treat while you spin it to occupy her.

- If she alerts to the incorrect container, just keep walking and ask her to continue checking. Do not punish her! Sometimes test her when she alerts to the correct container by continuing to walk around the wheel and asking her to continue checking other containers - reward her for staying at the correct container.

- If you want her to sit and paw the correct container, use the reward to lure her into a sit each time she stops at the correct container, then give the reward. If you don't care and just want her to paw, skip this and just reward at the scent source. (Clean compartments after each training session using a paper towel and hot water.)

- Vary the low samples you use during different training sessions. Only use 1 low sample at a time and never put a low sample in a different compartment in the wheel, to prevent accidental contamination.

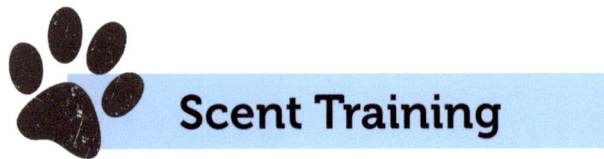
Scent Training

Step # __11__

Training Date(s):
_____

Location(s):
_____

Time(s) Spent:
_____

NOTES: _____

_____

_____

_____

_____

_____

_____

_____

_____

_____

_____

Scent Training

NOTES: _____

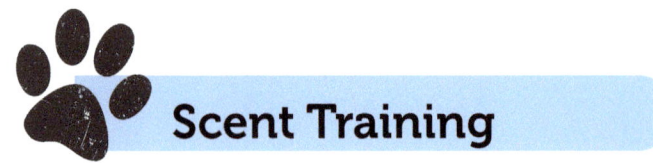

Step 12
Planned live alerts

Instructions:

When your blood sugar is low, wait near your dog to see if she recognizes the scent. If she shows any recognition at all (sitting up, starting to paw, etc.), ask her "What is it?" If she paws you, have a "Puppy Party" - give her 3 or 4 high value treats with lots of praise! If she doesn't show any recognition for 5 minutes, then practice Step 9 to pair the live low to the low sample. When she paws you, have a puppy party!

Repeat each time you are low and your dog has not alerted yet, for the rest of your dog's working life.

TIPS

- Quickly fade out asking, "What is it?" After a few repetitions let her think it through and paw you on her own, as you want her to be completely independent.

- Never let your blood sugar go low or high intentionally to practice. Your health is your priority. Only do this step if your blood sugar is in a safe enough range that you have time to walk by your dog before treating yourself.

Scent Training

Step # __12__

Training Date(s): _____

Location(s): _____

Time(s) Spent: _____

NOTES: _____

_____

_____

_____

_____

_____

_____

_____

_____

_____

_____

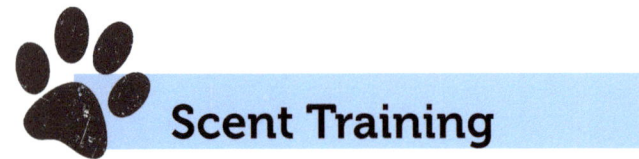

Scent Training

Step 13
Teaching high blood sugar alerts

Instructions:

Part A) Repeat Step 11 - Part A, but instead of a low sample, place one very high blood sugar sample (250mg/dL or above) in the wheel. ***Repeat approximately 10 times.***

Part B) Repeat Part A, but put in-range samples in the other wheel compartments. ***Repeat approximately 50 times, over multiple days.***

TIPS

- The purpose of this step is to teach your dog exactly what high blood sugars you want her to alert to. Most dogs begin to alert to extreme live high blood sugars on their own so this step is used to communicate the exact high alert threshold. But if your dog has not alerted to a live high blood sugar after a few months and you would like her to, practice this step to teach her that highs provide tasty treats as well!

- Vary the high blood sugar sample you place in the wheel to teach the dog to alert to any high blood sugar over a certain level. Practice with each sample approximately 10 times each training session. *During the next session use a different high sample. Use at least 30 different samples in total.*

- When dogs first alert to a live high blood sugar, they will typically be less confident and more hesitant. If you see your dog being particularly interested in you and sniffing you, but not being confident enough to paw, then check your blood sugar and if you are high, prompt her to alert to you, then have a party.

Scent Training

Step # __13__

Location(s): _____

Training Date(s): _____

Time(s) Spent: _____

NOTES: _____

_____

_____

_____

_____

_____

_____

_____

_____

_____

_____

Scent Training

Step 14
Independent live alerts

Instructions:

Any time your dog alerts on her own, say "Let's check", and immediately check your blood sugar. If she has alerted correctly, have a Puppy Party! Then say, "All better". If your blood sugar is normal, say "We'll watch" and continue about your business. Recheck every 10 minutes for the next 30 minutes. If you go out of range during those 30 minutes, then you can ask her to alert again ("What is it?") and have a party.

TIPS

- Many dogs will start live alerting before you are able to get through all of the previous 13 steps. Do not stop progressing through the steps! Keep going through the steps, performing all the repetitions in addition to rewarding for every verified live alert.

- If your dog correctly alerted, but your blood sugar level needs to be fixed immediately, say "Yes!" in an excited voice, quickly treat yourself, then have the Puppy Party. This communicates to the dog that their reward is coming, while making sure that you stay safe.

- "Let's check", "All better", and "We'll watch" all help to communicate with the dog. You can choose your own phrases instead of these, just be consistent.

- Sometimes glucose meters are incorrect – they only have to be within 20% of the correct reading. So if your dog is alerting persistently but the meter read that you were in-range, wash your hands thoroughly and recheck just in case.

Keep track of every alert or missed alert for the first 6 months of regular live alerting. A log for live alerting is in the "Records" section of the book. This can show trends and ways to improve your dog's alerting. (If you'd like to keep track on your phone, Google Sheets is very convenient and can be used on your phone or computer. Just create a log similar to the one in the records section.)

Scent Training

Step # __14__

Training Date(s): _____

Location(s): _____

Time(s) Spent: _____

NOTES: _____

_____

_____

_____

_____

_____

_____

_____

_____

_____

_____

_____

_____

Scent Training

Scent Training Pointers

- If you'd like to change your dog's alerting range (e.g. you want her to alert to 90 and below rather than 80 and below), follow Step 11 Part A, but place one sample of 90 in the scent wheel and leave the others blank. Revert back to rewarding for just a hesitation at the correct compartment, then gradually raise the criteria again. Repeat Step 11 Part C with the new levels.

- Switch up the 4 S's frequently - **Sample**, **Situation**, **Stance**, and **Schedule**.

- **Sample**: Don't always train with a sample of 80, practice with samples in the 50's, 60's and 70's as well.

- **Situation**: Practice everywhere you can think of – in the bedroom, in the bathroom, in the yard, in the car, in a train station, in a restaurant, in a school, at a fair, in a barn, etc.

- **Stance**: Practice in every position you can think of – sitting, standing, lying down on the bed, kneeling, lying on the ground, on a bench, while running, etc.

- **Schedule**: Practice at all different times of the day. If you practice scent training at just one time, the dog will false alert at that time of day as well as may not alert to live blood sugars because they won't expect it.

- Is Fido not live alerting? The most frequent reason is that the dog has not had sufficient practice alerting to hidden scent samples (Step 9). Before worrying, you should, at a minimum, complete the Scent Training Checklist located in the Records section of this book.

- Trust but verify. Trust that when your dog alerts, they are correct. However, do not reward unless your glucose meter can verify it. An example of 'trust but verify': Your dog alerts but your meter reads that you are in range. Rewash your hands and clean your finger with an alcohol wipe, then recheck to be sure the reading was accurate. Your dog won't always be right, that is normal! But never get frustrated or punish the dog for an alert that isn't correct. Just recheck every 10 minutes for 30 minutes.

- Always verify alerts with a finger stick and glucose meter, not a Continuous Glucose Monitor.

- Different glucose meter brands seem to run higher or lower than others. Be sure to always use the same brand when verifying alerts.

- Always be mindful of contamination – wash your hands before and after handling scent samples or containers of scent samples. Also, if a sample drops on the floor, on your clothing, or anywhere else, there is contamination. Clean it up as soon as possible to prevent the dog from being confused.

Scent Training

- Be realistic in your expectations. If you go to the dog park or somewhere very distracting, don't expect your dog to alert. If they do, fantastic! You have an incredible alerter! But don't be disappointed if your dog doesn't alert in that high distraction environment. That would be like asking you to take a math test in the stands of a football game among the cheering, food, people squeezing by your seat, cheerleaders, and a band. Sometimes it's okay to let your dog be a dog.

- Vary the treats your dog receives, even the high value treats. Dogs get bored of eating the same thing every day, so sometimes give your dog cheese, sometimes hotdogs, sometimes liver, etc. If it looks like your dog is losing excitement for alerts, it may be time to switch treats.

- Never reward the dog for a vocal alert. At the beginning of training your dog may get frustrated and bark when she is trying to alert but can't remember what to do. Stand still like a statue and do not say a thing. You do not want to encourage that behavior or it might become a habit and then will bark in public to alert, which is not appropriate.

- Trim your dog's nails every few days to minimize the scratches on your leg once they begin to alert to live out-of-range blood sugars.

- Typically less talking is better. Except when rewarding or working with the scent wheel, or if the dog is clearly struggling, do not give your dog a command or any prompting to find the scent or alert to it. We want the dog to be confident in detecting and responding to the scent without verbal cues.

- After training Steps 11 and 13, regularly do a blinded test (you do not know where the sample is located) so it is impossible that you inadvertently provide body language cues. Place the positive sample (low or high) in the wheel. Have another person know where the positive is and spin the wheel with you out of sight. The other person must watch where the positive lands then ask you to enter the room. Have your dog check the wheel and when she alerts, the other person should tell you whether she is correct or not. The purpose of this is to eliminate the possibility that you are unknowingly giving body language cues to your dog, showing her where to alert. Since you don't know where the low/high sample is, you can't tell your dog where it is. If your dog fails this multiple times, return to previous steps as most likely your dog doesn't understand her job.

- The more frequently you train, the better your dog will detect the scent of low or high blood sugars. This is actually based on science. As you train your dog, exposing her to the scent of low/high blood sugar and rewarding her for it, her brain is creating more connections resulting in the olfactory receptors increasing in number. When her olfactory receptors increase, she is better able to detect the out of range glucose levels.

- After Step 13, when you introduce high blood sugars, repeat Steps 8, 9, and 12 but with high samples. This will solidify your dog's understanding of alerting to highs as well.

False Alerts

False alerts are false positives - alerts the dog gives when the handler's blood sugar does not need alerting to. False alerts can occur for a variety of reasons, making it difficult to pinpoint the cause and even more difficult to determine the solution. Below are the most common reasons for false alerts as well as suggested solutions. Neither these causes nor the solutions are an exhaustive list as each dog and household is different, but a local trainer may be able to help you further if needed.

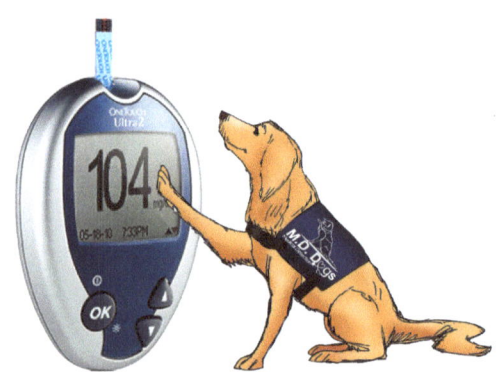

Reasons for false alerts:

SOMEONE ELSE IS LOW OR HIGH
(*not a false alert!)

- **Cause:** While as of this writing we do not know what substance the dogs are smelling when alerting to low or high blood sugars, the substance is constant between individuals so the dogs will initially typically alert to others who have low or high blood sugar. This is why organizations are able to train Diabetic Alert Dogs and then place them with individuals with diabetes - because the scent is not unique to each person. So when your dog is appearing to false alert, it could be that they are smelling another person's low or high blood sugar.

- **Solution:** It is up to each handler to decide if that is something that they reward the dog for, or if they want to untrain this. Typically it is best to not reward it, teaching the dog to only alert to their handler because this eliminates ambiguity. Many times it is not appropriate to ask someone if they might have low or high blood sugar, so you would not be able to confidently reward the alert, or confidently not reward it. Additionally, if you are in a conference setting, a church service, etc., it is not feasible to ask everyone around you, so again you would not know how to respond to the alert. Teaching the dog to only alert to the handler's low or high blood sugar takes time, but allows you to confidently know whether the dog's alert was correct and reward accordingly.

RAPID CHANGES
(*not a false alert!)

- **Cause:** Diabetic Alert Dogs trained only on scent samples above or below the desired alerting threshold (e.g. below 80mg/dL or above 180mg/dL) still usually learn to alert to rapid changes as well. Again, because we currently do not know what substance the dogs are alerting to, this could be due to the substance being emitted during

False Alerts

a rapid change when the samples are taken for a low or high blood sugar, or perhaps the dogs learn that a rapidly changing blood sugar results in a low or high so they preemptively alert.

- **Solution:** If rapid changes are something you would like the dog to alert to, then it is important to recheck every 10 minutes for 30 minutes after a supposed false alert. This is because by rechecking you are tracking your blood sugar and are able to see if the dog was alerting to a rapid drop or rise. (The definition of a rapid drop or rise varies based on each individual's criteria - some organizations utilize a change of 10% minimum, others require a change of 3mg/dL per minute. Whatever you decide to reinforce, ensure that you will not be bothered by rewarding every time you change by that amount. Keep in mind your rate of change when you give yourself insulin and when you eat, because the dogs will alert no matter the circumstances.)

EARLY ALERT
(*not a false alert!)

- **Cause**: Sometimes DADs will alert before you are low or high, but when you are trending that way. Perhaps you aren't changing rapidly, but you are slowly drifting towards their alerting threshold.

- **Solution:** Only reward for an alert when you are able to verify the accuracy with the meter. Recheck every 10 minutes for 30 minutes after an alert to ensure that your dog was not alerting in anticipation of a low or high. If during one of those rechecks you are low or high, in your dog's alerting range, then reward the dog - even if they didn't alert again. This reinforces the glucose levels they should alert at, as well as helps prevent them from becoming discouraged from their early alert not being rewarded. If your blood sugar never reaches the alerting threshold, then continue to go about your day without communicating anything to your dog.

METER INACCURACY
(*not a false alert!)

- **Cause:** According to the FDA (United States), 95% of a glucose meter's readings must be within 15% of the true lab value, and 99% must be within 20% of the true lab value. Meanwhile, we are asking the dogs to alert to exact thresholds, for example 80mg/dL and below. So how can we verify a dog's alert if the meter may even be incorrect? We do our best.

- **Solution:** The first step to take when your dog alerts and you are not within alerting range, is wash your hands and test again. If the results the second time are within the dog's alerting range, reward them! If your results are not within the alerting range, but are close you may also choose to reward them. Your criteria for "close to alerting range" is up to you. One suggestion is to always train with samples that are 80mg/dL, but reward for live alerts that are 85mg/dL and below. This is somewhat arbitrary and not based on meter variances, but helps to reward the dog as best as we can utilizing the tools we have.

False Alerts

ATTENTION SEEKING OR COMMUNICATION

- **Cause:** Some dogs naturally will paw, nudge, or stare when seeking attention or trying to communicate. This can easily become confused with an alert if you have chosen to train an alert behaviour that also comes naturally to the dog. For example, if you train a paw alert, and the dog learns it extremely quickly because they are so great with their paws, it means that there is also a risk that they use their paws to get pet. So when you are sitting on the couch and your dog comes up and places her paw on you it can be unclear whether she wants pet, wants outside, or whether you should test your blood sugar.

- **Solution:** The first step is to not pet your dog when they perform this behaviour. When they put their paw on you (or nudge, or any other alert behaviour), test your blood sugar first. If you think that it could be that the dog is wanting attention and not alerting, then definitely do not pet them to ensure you do not reinforce the behavior. While it may be natural for them to perform the behavior, petting them or giving them attention reinforces that the behavior may be used to achieve that goal. Instead, when you want to pet your dog, teach them an alternative behavior that they can use to communicate they'd like attention (for example: spin, bow, etc. any behavior that would not get confused with the alert). A second step that may be needed if the alert behavior confusion persists, is to add in a secondary alert. The secondary alert that is clearest is a bringsel. after adding in this secondary alert behavior, your dog will alert by pawing/nudging/etc. first, and then if you do not respond with what she intends, she will hold the bringsel, clearly demonstrating that you should check your blood sugar.

INSECURITY

- **Cause:** The goal of diabetic alert training is to cause the scent of out-of-range blood sugar as well as the action of alerting to be so reinforcing that the dog is constantly searching for the scent. A result of this though, is that sometimes the dogs view the alerting behavior as so reinforcing that they offer it at other times where they are uncertain of what to do. This can be seen frequently with dogs who are lacking in general confidence (ones who frighten at novel objects, become overstimulated in busy environments, bark at unknown sounds, etc.). This cause can be recognized because of the frequent false alerts when in public or stimulating environments, and a decrease of false alerts when at home or in known environments.

- **Solution:** There is no quick, easy, or guaranteed solution for this cause of false alerting. The best route is to build your dog's overall confidence in all situations and environments to minimize their insecurities so they do not resort to false alerting. However, this is a situation where if it cannot be fixed, the dog likely should remain an in-home Diabetic Alert Dog.

THRESHOLD CONFUSION

- **Cause:** We are asking the dogs to alert at specific thresholds of low and high

False Alerts

blood sugar - if you really think about this, it is remarkable! The ability for a dog to know the difference between 80mg/dL and 90mg/dL (for example) from scent alone is absolutely incredible. But this doesn't happen immediately and takes repetition for the dog to learn. While we don't fully understand how the dogs are able to alert, there is nothing special about the alert thresholds we choose, which is why you can choose any threshold your endocrinologist and you agree would be helpful. At the beginning of training, your dog has no reason to know that 80mg/dL and below is important, but anything above that is not. Your dog learns through hundreds, if not thousands, of repetitions, being rewarded when your blood sugar drops below the alerting threshold (or above) and not being rewarded when it is in a healthy range. So for the first few months of training your dog will of course alert when you are in a healthy range, because it takes time for them to learn what levels they get rewarded for.

- **Solution:** Training! Teaching the alerting threshold(s) is what training is for, so the more repetitions the better! Continue practicing with hidden scent samples frequently, practice with the scent wheel in training sessions, and continue rewarding all correct live alerts.

TRIAL AND ERROR

- **Cause:** When a dog is first learning to alert to glucose levels, they do a lot of trial and error so false alerts should occur! This is completely normal. To train a Diabetic Alert Dog, we are actually relying on our dog's ability to be a "furry scientist" - we train the dogs on saliva samples, yet they begin alerting to our live blood sugars despite it being quite a different smell than the samples we trained them with. If they didn't perform some trial and error, they would become superstars at alerting to samples but never alert to our actual low or high blood sugars, making terrible Diabetic Alert Dogs! (This experimentation is also how DADs learn to alert to high blood sugars on their own, which is incredible!)

- **Solution:** When your dog false alerts for unknown reasons, it is likely it is due to this trial and error period, especially if its within 6-12 months of the start of their training. Respond by checking your blood sugar, rechecking every 10 minutes for 30 minutes to ensure the alert was not due to any of the other reasons, and then continue about your day, not rewarding the dog but also never correcting them for an incorrect alert. We rely on the dogs to have the confidence to experiment which enables them to transition from samples to live alerts, and from low blood sugar alerts to high blood sugar alerts; but along with this comes false alerts as they attempt to alert in other situations for other reasons. This is completely normal, just have patience and consistency and over the next months your dog will realize what she is rewarded for and what is not worthy of alerting to.

Walking Alerts

Walking Alerts

Walking alerts are just that - alerts while walking. They often take additional training because the physical mechanics can be difficult for a dog to work out and they often need to be taught how to alert in that type of situation. Prior to having been taught a walking alert, a DAD will start to either forge ahead or lag behind when they smell an out of range blood sugar level, but when the dog is still in training this can easily be misinterpreted as the dog failing to heel correctly. Because of this, usually the handler never gives it a second thought and responds as if they have temporarily forgotten their manners and appropriate heel position, so the dog is taught to essentially not alert while walking.

Teaching a walking alert early on can help eliminate some confusion and frustration, as well as minimize missed alerts.

Walking Alerts

Step 1

With an out-of-range scent sample in hand, but in an airtight container, ask your dog to heel and begin walking (ideally in a straight line, down the neighborhood block, for example). Then while walking, open the scent sample and place it at your dog's nose height right against your leg. This should allow your dog to heel next to you and sniff the sample easily. When your dog acknowledges the sample, mark and reward with multiple treats and lots of praise! (Acknowledgment would be them sniffing it, wiggling all over in excitement suddenly, jumping on you, etc.). Repeat approximately 3 times.

Step 2

Repeat Step 1, but as your dog offers various behaviors to communicate, wait for a behaviour that you would like as your walking alert. When your dog performs the behavior, mark and reward while continuing to walk and allowing them to repeat the behavior until they have done it about 3-5 times, being rewarded each time. This walking alert behaviour does not at all need to be the same as their stationary alert behavior. The goal is to have an alert that is clear and convenient, as well as not dangerous to you or the dog. Recommended walking alerts: nudging the back of the handler's leg with their nose, or slight jumping on the back of the handler's leg. Repeat approximately 5 times.

Step 3

Repeat Step 2, but rub the scent sample on your hand closest to your dog rather than holding a container with the scent sample inside. This more closely mimics a live alert. Repeat approximately 3 times.

Step 4

Repeat Step 2, but without the dog noticing and in a new training session, discreetly rub the scent sample on your hand in the middle of a walk that is 5 minutes or longer. The goal is to mimic a real situation where your dog suddenly smells the low or high blood sugar and alerts you while walking. Repeat as many times as needed until your dog confidently alerts while walking next to you.

Night Alerts

Night Alerts

Night alerts are one of the most difficult aspects of DAD training, and not every DAD will be capable of alerting at night. Additionally, night alerts will never replace night time glucose checks and the dogs do not work like machines, magically waking up as soon as you drop below or above their alerting threshold. Night alerts usually occur when the dog is at the most conscious part of their sleep cycle, or they are shifting positions and are aware enough to recognize the scent. Because of this, it is critical you never rely on a dog for night alerts.

However, by practicing frequently and altering the context of night alerts, you can maximize the chance that your dog will learn to alert at night. Below are suggestions to increase your dog's night alerts:

Include your dog in the process.

The first step is to include the dog in your typical night checking process. Each time you wake up to check your blood sugar, wake your dog up and get them excited enough to come with you to check, or aware that you are checking. Then if you are low or high, have a party! It doesn't matter if your dog did or did not alert, just begin to create that positive association and show your dog that puppy parties happen at night too!

Practice the mechanics.

Exactly like Step 9 of scent training (alerting based on scent alone), except practice when in bed lying down, mimicking your position when sleeping at night. Then reward the dog for alerting in a manner that would successfully wake you up. Frequently night alerts are not the same as day alerts - dogs will sometimes lay on your chest, jump on and off the bed repeatedly, or dig at the blankets. These are all excellent choices and perfectly

Night Alerts

acceptable because the goal is to be effective and safe. Let your dog decide what type of alert is natural to them while you are in that position, and then reward them when they demonstrate a natural alerting behaviour that also fits your needs.

Scent sample practice at night.

Replicate Step 9 of scent training, but at night. This will mimic night alerts as best as possible. The complicated part of this is remaining awake, or waking up in the middle of the night without waking your dog up as well. Initially you can set an alarm to wake you up so you can open the scent sample and practice alerts, however your dog will quickly learn to alert based on the alarm. So before this occurs, you will have to find another way to wake up in the middle of the night. One suggestion is to set a vibrate only alarm on your smartwatch so that your dog will not wake up to it but you will. Or, a low-tech method is to drink a few glasses of water prior to going to bed and letting nature wake you up ☺ This is not the most comfortable method but definitely will not wake your dog up!

Alter their sleeping location.

When trying to train night alerts, make sure your dog is sleeping in close enough proximity that the scent of the diabetic handler will be strong. The dog should definitely be in the same room as the diabetic, but does not need to sleep in bed with them. Also keep in mind fan directions and air flow in your house.

Change their bed.

Another way to help your dog alert more frequently at night is to use a bed that will cause them to shift a little more. Rather than having multiple fluffy blankets, try just a dog cot. They may shift a few more times at night, which will then allow them to be aware enough to recognize an out of range blood sugar and alert, thus earning their puppy party.

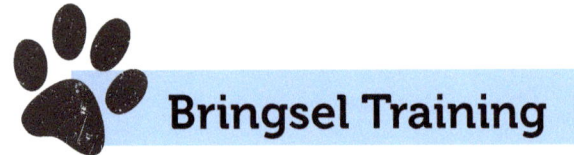

Bringsel Training

Bringsel Training

While paw alerts ensure that you are aware of your dog's presence, sometimes they can be a little ambiguous. Dogs that are naturally paw oriented will learn the paw alert in scent training sessions very quickly, however those same dogs will also tend to use their paw for other communication because it is natural for them. For example when she wants affection she may place her paw on your arm, or when she needs outside she may attempt to place her paw on your lap. This can cause confusion, unnecessary glucose testing, and lead to frustration because she either appears to be false alerting or appears to be missing alerts.

All DAD training requires reading your dog's body language and signs, but one way to make it a little easier is to add in a secondary alert that is a very unnatural behavior for your dog, such as a bringsel hold. In DAD training, a bringsel is a tab that the dog holds when they are alerting to your low or high glucose levels.

Bringsel training is not for the faint of heart, and often requires frequent troubleshooting. Not every dog needs to be, or even should be, taught a bringsel alert. Paw alerts and nudge alerts are frequently just as effective and are easier to teach because they do not require an additional variable which complicates scent training. If you are new to training or not confident in problem solving, focus on paw or nudge alerts alone, or consult a trainer during bringsel training to ensure your dog's existing alerting abilities are not compromised.

Types of Bringsels

There are two types of bringsels. One type are velcro retrieval bringsels - typically a stuffed canvas tube which has velcro on the end and hangs on the handler's belt loops as well as in certain locations around the house. The dog pulls the bringsel and brings it to the handler.

The second type of bringsel is one that hangs on the dog's collar at all times and the dog picks it up in their mouth to alert. MD Dogs designed a bringsel of this type, specifically to easily clip on and off the dog's collar and made of biothane so they can be easily cleaned by wiping them down to prevent dirt and bacteria from accumulating. The benefit to MD Dogs' bringsels is that the bringsel is always available to the dog in the same location and does not rely on the handler's wardrobe including belt loops, or on bringsels being hung around the room. However, if you prefer the velcro retrieval bringsels, then the following instructions can be modified accordingly.

Bringsel Training

Sizing an MD Dogs Bringsel

The width of a bringsel typically has little effect on the ease of use. There are two widths for an MD Dogs bringsel - ⅝ inch and ½ inch. The ⅝ inch bringsel may be a little easier for the dog to hold, but will be slightly cumbersome on a small breed, while the ½ inch tends to curve a little if it is long for a large dog. But both are effective!

The length of a bringsel is much more important than the width. Too short of a bringsel will be difficult for the dog to grab, causing them to possibly give up on using it, however too long of a bringsel risks that the dog will step on it throughout the day. To determine the right length, measure from where your dog's collar sits to the top of your dog's breastbone (this protrudes from the rest of their chest). Multiply this measurement by two, and this is the length of the MD Dogs bringsel to order! Example: Beni's collar-to-breastbone measurement is 3", so the 6" bringsel is perfect for him. (This is only applicable for MD Dogs branded bringsels by CSJcreations, not those sold by any other store due to sizing differentiations.)

Training The Bringsel Alert

Introduce the bringsel after your dog has reached Step 9 of scent training and is successfully alerting to hidden scent samples. This is because if we begin bringsel training too early on, then there will be more value for the bringsel than the scent of low blood sugar, and the dog will hold the bringsel, appearing to false alert, but not because they are confused about the scent of low blood sugar but because they are hoping to receive a puppy party.

Unlike in the scent training steps, during bringsel training if your dog moves on to the next step before all the repetitions are completed, that is completely okay! Mark and reward it! For example, if you are on Step 1 when she attempts to put the bringsel in her mouth, mark and reward it immediately because that's what we'd like her to do. Then repeat it again and if she puts it in her mouth again, mark and reward and continue with Step 2. If she only investigates, then that's okay too; just continue with Step 1 until she offers the behavior of putting it in her mouth again.

When rewarding your dog, incorporate praise when they first progress to another step - this will help her move to the next step as well as keep her excited and motivated. Also to help increase drive, toss treats a few feet away from you when rewarding.

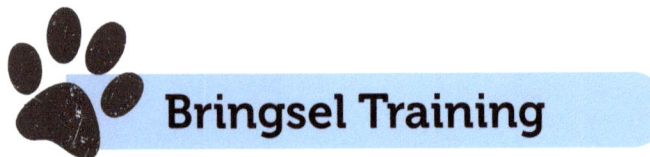

Bringsel Training

Step 1

Bringsel investigation

While at your dog's level (kneeling, sitting on the ground, or sitting in a chair) hold the bringsel in your hand and present it in front of the dog. When she investigates it mark and reward. *Repeat approximately 20 times.*

Step 2

Bringsel in mouth

Hold the bringsel in your hand and present it in front of the dog. When she makes contact with her mouth mark and reward. *Repeat approximately 40 times.*

Step 3

Bringsel investigation on ground

Place the bringsel on the ground in front of the dog. When she investigates it, mark and reward. Then begin to reward only when she goes to pick it up. *Repeat approximately 15 times.*

Step 4

Bringsel pick up

Place the bringsel on the ground in front of the dog. When she picks it up all the way, mark and reward. *Repeat approximately 30 times.*

Step 5

Bringsel hold short duration

Place the bringsel on the ground in front of the dog. When she picks it up all the way, wait 1 second and then mark and reward. *Gradually increase the time she must hold it before you mark and reward, until you reach 3 seconds.*

Because we often teach the dogs through shaping where they learn to offer a different behavior if they are not rewarded quickly, provide feedback to your dog as they are holding the bringsel so that they understand they are doing well and should continue holding it. I count out loud as my communication to continue holding. For example toward the end of this step my verbal communication to

Bringsel Training

the dog sounds like this: *"1 mississippi, 2 mississippi, 3 mississippi. Yes! Good job, Fido!"* and when I say "Yes!" I am also presenting a food reward.

If she drops it at any point, just give her a negative marker word in a neutral tone and wait for her to try again. (do *not* sound discouraging - a negative marker word is purely to communicate that she doesn't get a reward for that and should try again). If she drops it a few times in a row, return to the previous step or end the session and try again later. *Repeat as many times as needed until she picks it up and holds it for 3 seconds routinely.*

Step 6

Adding the verbal cue

After practicing Step 5 a few times, place the bringsel on the ground again and at the same time give your verbal cue you'd like to use so she pairs the verbal cue with the behavior of holding the bringsel for 3 seconds. Example cues: *"Bringsel"*, *"Hold"*, or *"Alert"*. *Repeat approximately 5 times.*

Step 7

Bringsel hold long duration

Repeat Step 5, but working from a 3 second hold up to a 10 second hold and incorporating her verbal cue each time she is about to pick up the bringsel. *Repeat as many times as needed until she picks it up and holds it for 10 seconds routinely.*

Step 8

Generalize the bringsel hold

Instead of being at your dog's level, stand up and drop the bringsel on the ground and give her bringsel verbal cue. When she picks it up mark and reward. *Repeat approximately 5 times.*

Step 9

Generalize the bringsel hold long duration

Repeat Step 8, but work up to the dog holding the bringsel for 10 seconds routinely; gradually increase the duration to set her up for success. Again use

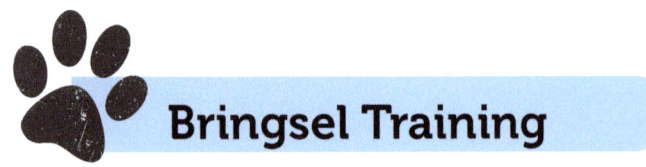

Bringsel Training

any verbal communication needed to encourage her to continue holding it, and over time you can fade the verbal communication out. *Repeat as many times as needed until she picks up the bringsel and holds it for 10 seconds.*

Step 10

Bringsel hold with handler movement

While standing, place the bringsel on the ground and give the dog the verbal cue to hold it. Then take a few steps while giving verbal communication for the dog to continue holding it. After just a few steps and about 3 seconds, mark and reward! Gradually increase the duration and the steps you take, teaching the dog to continue holding the bringsel no matter where you are or what you are doing. Work up to the dog holding the bringsel while you walk for 10 seconds in any direction or movement pattern. *Repeat as many times as needed.*

Step 11

Vertical bringsel hold

While at your dog's level again (kneeling, sitting, or on a chair), hold the bringsel from the clip end, so it is dangling vertically in front of the dog. Give the "bringsel" cue and when she puts it in her mouth, mark and reward. *Repeat approximately 5 times.*

Step 12

Bringsel hold from collar attempt

In the same training session as practicing Step 11, clip the bringsel to the dog's collar. Give the verbal cue and when she attempts to hold it, mark and reward. *Repeat approximately 3 times.*

Step 13

Bringsel hold from collar success

Repeat Step 12, but wait until she successfully holds it in her mouth. When she does successfully hold it, mark and reward with praise! *Repeat approximately 10 times.*

Bringsel Training

Step 14

Bringsel hold from collar duration

Repeat Step 13, but gradually increase the duration of the bringsel hold, utilizing the same verbal communication you used in Step 5. *Repeat until she routinely holds the bringsel hanging on her collar for up to 10 seconds.*

Step 15

Preparing to pair the scent and bringsel

Thaw a low blood sugar scent sample and place it in a tin, and clip the bringsel to the dog's collar. While at your dog's level, present the tin to the dog. Mark and reward her for sniffing the tin (if she gives the previously taught indication such as nudging, pawing, etc. that's completely okay as well). *Repeat only 3 times.*

Step 16

Pairing the scent and bringsel

With two rewards in your hand and directly after Step 15, present the tin again in front of the dog. Give the first reward when she sniffs the tin, and then immediately give the "bringsel" cue. When she holds the bringsel, mark and reward with the second treat. *Repeat approximately 20 times.*

*If she gets frustrated and repeatedly sniffs or indicates on the scent tin rather than holding the bringsel, reward intermittently to avoid accidentally untraining her response to low blood sugar. Just also continue asking for the bringsel hold as well.

*If she begins to hold the bringsel without sniffing the tin, withhold the reward until she goes to acknowledge the tin again.

Step 17

Generalize the sniff and hold

Repeat Step 16 but hold the sample tin at different locations - to the left of your body, to the right of your body, behind your back, etc. This teaches the dog to find the scent source, sniff it, and hold the bringsel. At this stage also begin to fade out the bringsel cue, waiting for her to offer it on her own. Repeat approximately 20 times.

Step 18

Incorporating the bringsel hold to hidden scent samples

Repeat Step 9 of scent training (hiding a scent sample on your body). When the dog locates the scent sample, mark and reward. Then wait for her to hold the bringsel, and mark and reward again. Repeat regularly throughout your dog's working life.

Troubleshooting

Bringsel as a toy

When you first place the bringsel on your dog's collar, many will attempt to use it as a toy. This is normal! Leave lots of more fun toys lying around your dog at all times during this stage, and if she tries to use the bringsel as a toy just redirect her attention to a more fun one. This behavior will be extinguished as long as each time she attempts to play with it she is redirected. Also, at this stage do not leave the bringsel on the dog's collar when she is not being supervised. If she is left free to chew on it when bored, it will become reinforcing to her and a habit that will be much more difficult to extinguish.

Bringsel as an offered behavior

During the first few weeks or months of bringsel training your dog will be reinforced for holding the bringsel. Because of this, she will likely often offer it as a behavior when she is uncertain what to do. If you are teaching her a new behavior, especially through shaping (for explanation of shaping see *Puppy Steps* book), take the bringsel off her collar so she cannot engage in offering the behavior. This will eliminate frustration as well as reinforce to her that the bringsel is only used when alerting to low or high blood sugar.

Chomping on the bringsel

If your dog is mouthy when holding - beginning at step 5, do not reward until she stops mouthing it and just calmly holds it.

Scent Training

M.D. Dogs Inc
Diabetic Alert Dog Training Steps
Scent Games

Scent Games

Catch Me If You Can!

When? After you have completed all 14 scent training steps and she is confidently pawing you to alert to low blood sugars.

Purpose? To teach her to be confident in alerting you no matter your situation.

Pull out a scent sample and wait for her to alert. (Can also be done when you have a live low or high blood sugar).

When the dog alerts, mark and reward, but only once. Then the next time she tries to alert, hop backwards in a playful manner so that she misses and can't paw you. Then the next time, repeat it but hop back a little less and let her paw you. When she does, mark and reward.

Repeat this but start making it more difficult, running backwards from her, dodging her pawing behavior until she catches you. Make sure to always let her win after a few attempts and to keep it fun and upbeat with big rewards as soon as she does make contact with your leg. Do 8-10 repetitions before saying "All better" and ending the game.

Scent Games

Hide, Seek, and Alert

When? After you have completed all 14 scent training steps and have practiced the Catch Me If You Can! game.

Purpose? To teach her to be confident in alerting you no matter your situation.

After you've played the game, Catch Me If You Can! a few different times, you can make it more difficult by positioning yourself in more obscure locations as well as hiding when you open a scent sample or when your blood sugar is low or high.

Open a scent sample and wait for her to alert. When she does, mark and reward excitedly once. But then go to an obscure location or stand in an obscure position such as standing on your bed or desk. Then wait for her to alert. Choose the positions you practice wisely, for example standing on your bed is a great way to practice night alerts. You can use this as an opportunity to teach her that she doesn't get a puppy party unless she physically makes contact with you, even if that means jumping on the bed. This will help ensure she is able to wake

Scent Games

you up at night. At first she might just paw the bed, but that's okay. Wait for her to use her brain and figure out how to get to you, then as soon as she does mark and reward. When you reward, toss the treat on the ground away from the bed, so that she jumps off to get the treat, then has to use what she has just learned in order to alert again.

Once she is successfully able to alert you when you are standing somewhere that she can't reach, start visually hiding from her. Let her alert you once normally, then toss the treat on the ground away from you. While she runs to eat it, hide behind a slightly opened door (closet doors work great). She will have seen where you went, and that's okay. Wait for her to think about how to alert you. If she reaches her paw in or if she paws the door, reward and toss a treat out. Then wait for her to come back and alert again, then reward again. Repeat this until she is very confident and you can say "All better", and end the game.

Keep trying to think of new ways to challenge her alerting skills. The more you practice the better she will be at generalizing her alerting behavior so that she alerts no matter what you are doing or where you are!

Public Access

M.D. Dogs Inc
Diabetic Alert Dog Training Steps

Socialization & Public Access

Public Access

The Difference Between Socialization and Public Access Training

The difference between socialization and public access training is that socialization teaches your dog to be confident and curious, while public access training teaches her to ignore everything around her and focus on you. Begin with socialization and gradually add in public access training. As your dog matures and improves, add more public access training and decrease socialization training (a chart is on the page following this section). This schedule maximizes the puppy's critical socialization window, while also teaching her how to behave in public from an early age.

Socialization

Socialization is the process of exposing your puppy to various objects, people, places, and sounds, and teaching her to adapt in a way that builds confidence. The reason this is done with puppies is because they have a critical socialization period until about 4 months of age. This is why it is crucial to begin socializing your puppy as soon as you bring her home. It is still possible to socialize a dog after 4 months of age, but it is exponentially more difficult and time consuming, and at that point some fears may be permanent.

To socialize your puppy, take her to pet friendly stores such as Lowe's, Home Depot, and Tractor Supply Co. Always ask if a store is pet friendly because

Public Access

some store policies vary by location. When you take your puppy out, practice some obedience commands and walk with her a little, but if she gets tired feel free to pick her up or place her in the cart if the store allows it. The primary purpose is to let her hear all the sounds, see big machines, see different people, and smell new scents.

Since you have a puppy, people will want to pet her! You can allow people to pet her if you choose, but you don't need to actively seek people out or ask them to give her treats unless she shows hesitancy. The goal at this age is to build her confidence and ensure everything that happens in these environments is fun and exciting.

If your puppy is scared or unsure of anything or anyone, practice the Jolly Routine (page 35 of *Puppy Steps*). For a checklist of exposure items, visit the Resources section in the back of this book.

When socializing, never put a vest on your puppy. When the puppy begins public access training, she will begin to wear the vest and naturally associate the vest with ignoring everything around her. If she wears the vest while being socialized, then the vest will not have this same association.

Public Access Training

Public access training entails taking your DAD in training into non-pet friendly stores while she wears her vest. (Legally she does not have to wear a vest, but it is not fair to expect the public to treat your dog as a service dog if she is not labeled as such). Not every state in the United States gives service dogs in training and owner trainers public access rights. Check your state laws prior to taking your DAD in training in public. If your state does not give you and your dog those rights, that is okay. It is still very possible to prepare your dog for service work, it will just take more intentional trips to pet friendly stores rather than being able to practice public access training in any store. Do the same exercises and put your dog's service vest on, even though you are in pet friendly stores. (You can ask stores individually if they would allow you to train your dog in their stores as they will frequently give teams in training permission.)

Once your puppy knows the commands listed in the "Checklist Prior to Beginning Public Access", you can begin her public access training. These trips should be very short at first (5 minutes or less) and consist of heeling into the store, performing a few commands,

Public Access

perhaps walking around a little, and then leaving. The reason for this length is to keep it so short that your pup just gets a glimpse of public access training, and wants more.

Throughout the entire time actively engage your dog. Now is not the time to pick up the groceries your forgot to buy earlier. Focus solely on your puppy. When heeling, praise her and give her treats for watching you and ignoring everything around her. Your eyes should be on her the entire time at this stage and the second you see her sniff something or attempt to pull at the leash, respond by becoming more engaging so that you are so much more exciting than the items on the shelf or crumbs on the ground. If she learns that she is allowed to sniff objects, eat food, and not focus on you, then she will not be paying attention to your blood sugar levels, which is the reason she is with you.

As your pup succeeds, begin to gradually increase the duration of public access trips. And as your pup becomes more experienced (after a few months usually) you can also decrease the constant engagement with her and begin to focus on shopping, but always revert back if you notice your dog's behavior in public declining.

Starting public access training with short but focused sessions when your pup is young, results in a dog that has never known anything other than public access and thinks that you are the only person in the world that matters.

Public Access

Socialization and Public Access Timeline

When your puppy is 8 weeks old socialization trips should typically be 5 minutes or less, and every week thereafter can be about 5 minutes longer. Similarly, at 13 weeks public access trips should be 5 minutes or less, and every week thereafter can be 5 minutes longer. By 16 weeks, socialization outings could be up to 45 minutes and public access trips could be 20 minutes. If your puppy ever seems overwhelmed or is not enjoying socialization or public access outings, stop both socialization and public access and seek a trainer in your area to help. You can always go at a slower pace than suggested below as it is preferable to build a solid foundation and each dog progresses at its own rate. These guidelines are the fastest recommended progression even with a phenomenal puppy.

Below is an example schedule of socialization and public access trips a DAD puppy may experience as she matures.

8 WEEKS
- Socialization – Lowe's
- Socialization – Tractor Supply Co
- Socialization – Farmer's Market

9 WEEKS
- Socialization – Home Depot
- Socialization – Southern States
- Socialization – Car dealership

10 WEEKS
- Socialization – Family reunion
- Socialization – Outdoor restaurant
- Socialization – Lowe's

11 WEEKS
- Socialization – 4 hour road trip
- Socialization – Outdoor restaurant
- Sociazliation – Home Depot
- Socialization – Friend's house

12 WEEKS
- Socialization – 5 hour car ride
- Socialization – Tractor Supply Co
- Socialization – Outdoor cafe
- Socialization – Famer's Market

13 WEEKS
- Socialization – Outdoor concert
- Socialization - Lowe's
- Socialization – Outdoor cafe
- Public Access – Lowes

14 WEEKS
- Socialization – Vet appointment
- Socialization – Outdoor cafe
- Public Access – Farmer's Market
- Public Access – Indoor restaurant

15 WEEKS
- Socialization – 10 hour car ride
- Public Access – Indoor mall
- Public Access – Cafe
- Public Access – Grocery store

16 WEEKS
- Socialization – Vet appointment
- Public Access – Restaurant
- Public Access –Walmart
- Public Access – Grocery store
- Public Access –Indoor mall
- Pass AKC's Canine Good Citizen

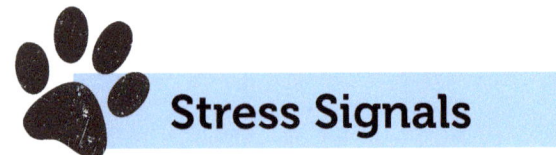

Stress Signals

Public access is very difficult on a dog so it is important to always be watching for stress signals that communicate your dog is uncomfortable. Puppies and adolescents go through fear periods; during these times they will show more uncertainty and it is imperative to recognize these signals and work the dog through their uncertainty rather than try to push through it without building up their confidence, as that can cause a dog to be too afraid in public to do its job.

The following are signs to be aware of. Many of these behaviors can occur in situations other than when the dog is stressed as well, so don't panic if you notice these behaviors. Continue watching your dog closely and when you see the dog demonstrating the behaviors frequently or in specific situations, counteract the fear. Some fears cannot be overcome, but if you are able to recognize and address these stress signals at the beginning, you will decrease the likelihood that the dog will need to be washed out from DAD training.

Stress signals are not always bad, they can be a coping mechanism and demonstrate that a dog is thinking. For example, some of the stress signals occur prior to an alert, called pre-alerts. Stretching and yawning are the two most common pre-alerts. If your dog does these behaviors prior to an alert, this is normal. But in general, just be aware of stress signals and if they are frequently occurring in certain situations then work with your dog to make it a positive experience and overcome the fear.

SHAKING OFF – Sometimes a dog needs to shake off to readjust her vest or set her fur back in place. But if a dog shakes off at what appears to be random times, it may be a sign of stress.

YAWNING – If a dog has been sleeping or resting for a while, a yawn or two is normal. But if she yawns when she has not been resting recently, she may be unsure of something around her.

LIP LICKING – Lip licking may occur when you give your dog treats for good behavior, but if it occurs when no treats have been given recently, it may be a sign of stress. This signal is generally demonstrated when she is stressed about one thing in particular rather than public access as a whole.

Stress Signals

SCRATCHING – An occasional scratch is normal, but if the dog stops walking to scratch, scratches while walking, or repeatedly scratches while under a table, she is likely stressed. This behavior is usually shown when she is stressed about public access in general rather than stressed about one particular object.

STRETCHING – Sometimes stretching will occur after the dog has been sleeping or in tight quarters, purely to extend their muscles. But it is also one of the most common stress signals and will also occur when the dog is unsure of the situation, or as a pre-alert.

PANTING – If it is hot outside, the dog has a thick coat, or the dog has been active then panting can occur without being a sign of stress. If your dog does not normally pant, but pants frequently when in public, it is likely a sign that she is uncomfortable in public.

TREMBLING – If a dog is trembling when in public, she is very stressed and should likely not be considered as a DAD candidate. While it is possible to overcome some stress, it would be prudent to use a different dog because a DAD needs to have confidence in all situations, despite constant stressful experiences. Trembling is such an extreme stress signal that it may be difficult to completely overcome and have the dog alert reliably and truly relax in public.

WHINING – A service dog should be silent in public; if it whines then it may be a sign that it is stressed. Whining could also be a way to communicate that it needs to relieve itself or is a pre-alert. Be careful to not encourage whining as a way to communicate anything, but if you do notice it and think it is a stress signal then be sure to try to counteract it.

BARKING – A service dog should not bark in public. If the dog barks, it may be because it is unsure about something. Typically this is in response to a particular object or sound.

DROPPED OR TUCKED TAIL – The goal is for public access to be fun for the dog, so it's ideal if their tail is raised because they enjoy working. If the dog's tail is dropped, it may be a sign of stress. Often this will not cause a dog to be washed out of Diabetic Alert Dog training, but if you can notice it and counteract it from the beginning by

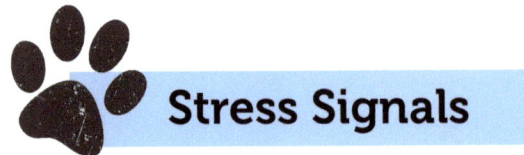

Stress Signals

making public access a fun and positive experience, then the dog will likely learn to love public access work.

SNIFFING GROUND – A service dog should not sniff the ground or objects while vested. If a dog begins to sniff after being trained not to, it may be a way to cope with the stress of public access work. If the dog is sniffing in places such as the meat aisle, then it is likely not stress and she just needs some additional leave it practice 8.

DROOLING – Some breeds naturally drool in all situations. If that's the case, this would not be considered a stress signal. But for the majority of breeds, drooling is a signal of stress. Drooling would typically be in response to public access in general rather than one specific object/sound/etc.

Public Access

Public Access Guidelines (when in the United States)

 The dog should be on the ground at all times. It should not be in a cart, held, carried, on a chair, etc. This is a courtesy to those around you. A dog should not be in the cart because that's where people put their items and some may not appreciate dog fur or placing items where dog feet have been. The Americans with Disabilities Act FAQ says that service dogs can be carried if it's a dog that detects scents on the breath and it gives the example of a DAD. However, a DAD does not need to be that close to alert and it is unprofessional for the dog to be carried, even if it is small. Small service dogs need to have the same high standards as large service dogs. But the good news is that small dogs are just as trainable as medium or large dogs, and a well-behaved, small DAD will be an excellent representation of the capabilities of small dogs.

 Your goal is to have your dog go unnoticed. She should be silent, well groomed, and well behaved at all times.

 Some people may challenge your access rights. If you are in a public place, your dog is fully trained (or in training and you are in a state that allows in training service dogs access), and your dog is being well behaved, then you have the right to enter that business. However, even with access issues, always be professional and courteous. Do not raise your voice, yell, or get worked up. Try to show or explain the Americans with Disabilities Act or state laws and if that does not work, calmly offer to call the police to have the issue resolved. The key is calmly. You are representing all service dogs. When service dog handlers yell and threaten to sue businesses, we are actually hurting ourselves because then the businesses become so wary of service dogs that they fail to ask anyone about any dog brought into their business, enabling fake service dog teams to enter more easily.

 If your dog ever shows aggression of any type or relieves herself in public more than twice, remove your dog from all public access training until you are able to understand and fix the behavior entirely.

 Always have a non-retractable leash on your dog. The dog can be off leash if it interferes with their task, but if your dog is just trained to be a DAD a leash does not interfere.

 A service dog should never interfere with items or people around her. She should never be sniffing items, the floor, or people, or soliciting attention. Her attention should always be on her handler.

Public Access

Checklist Prior to Beginning Public Access

Before beginning any public access training, your puppy should know at least the following commands with 90% success rate, both at home and in pet friendly stores.

- ☐ Sit
- ☐ Down
- ☐ Sit Stay (Distance - 5 feet)
- ☐ Down Stay (Distance – 5 feet)
- ☐ Come (Come and sit in front of me)
- ☐ Heel (Walk at my left side on a loose leash)
- ☐ Close (Sit at my left side)
- ☐ Place (Duration – 30 seconds)
- ☐ Watch Me (give me eye contact)
- ☐ Leave It
- ☐ Get Dressed
- ☐ Powder Your Nose (relieve herself)

🐾 Use lots of treats and praise during public access training. Your puppy should think that you are the only thing that matters in public because you are far more fun than the environment around her!

🐾 Always make sure your puppy relieves herself prior to entering a store. If your puppy is less than 4 months old and doesn't relieve herself prior to going in a store, do not enter the store in order to minimize the risk of an accident. (If going on a socialization outing this is still a good idea, but because your dog isn't labeled as a service dog and you would be entering a pet friendly establishment it is not as essential.)

🐾 Remember: Anytime you are out with your pup in a vest (or in a non-pet friendly place), you are representing all service dogs. Be respectful of the rights you are given and ensure your puppy is professional at all times. If you are unsure if your puppy is being professional, leave the establishment and continue practicing at home and in pet friendly stores to solidify her obedience before labeling her as a service dog in training.

Public Access

Checklist of Total Obedience Commands

A DAD should be inconspicuous and out of the way when in public. This is a list of suggested commands your DAD should know by the completion of training so you can keep her safe and be respectful of the public.

- Sit
- Down
- Stand
- Sit Stay (distance – 25 feet)
- Down Stay (distance – 25 feet)
- Stand Stay (distance – 5 feet)
- Come
- Heel (walk at my left side, sit when I stop)
- Close (sit at my left side)
- Side (sit at my right side)
- Between (sit between my feet)
- Front (down between wall and my feet)
- Behind (down between a wall and my heels)
- Go On (walk in front me)
- Follow (walk behind me)
- Place (duration – 4 hours)
- Watch Me
- Leave It
- Touch
- Under
- Paws Up (front two paws on object)
- Get Up (back two paws on object)
- Get Dressed
- Break
- Off
- Powder Your Nose (relieve herself)
- Chill (put chin on my foot)
- Get Juice
- Get the Meter

Copyrighted Information

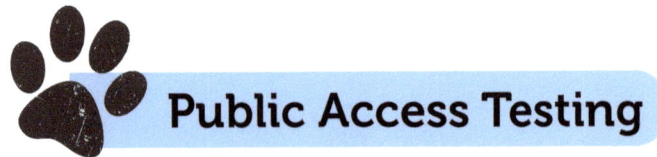

MD Dogs Public Access Test (PAT)

TEST INTENT: The MD Dogs PAT assesses a service dog team's ability to maneuver in public in a manner that is safe, professional, and courteous to those around them. It also assesses the dogs ability to perform its medical alert task in a busy, natural environment, demonstrating its qualifications to have public access as a service dog (in countries with such laws, such as the United States). This test's purpose is to help guide those who are training their own dogs, providing tangible goals and exercises to practice; to help a team decide if they are ready to transition from "in training" to "fully trained"; and lastly, is a required portion of the voluntary MD Dogs Verification for medical alert dog teams. (To learn more visit MDdogs.org).

Minimum Qualifications: The dog must be at least 12 months of age when taking this test. You can practice these exercises prior to 12 months, but be sure to demonstrate the entire test after 12 months of age to demonstrate your dog's ability to professionally work in public as an adolescent or adult.

Disqualification and removal: If the dog demonstrates aggression of any type (growling, raised hackles, biting, showing teeth, etc.) or relieves itself indoors the dog will be disqualified and should be removed from the public.

Location: This test should be performed in an indoor mall or shopping center with numerous people and natural distractions, with access to the following: food court, a store with shopping carts, and at least two floors.

Equipment: The handler may utilize any reasonable and humane equipment with the exception of retractable leashes. The evaluator will need a clipboard and scent sample.

Evaluator/Assistant: Ideally the evaluator would be an experienced service dog trainer who can discreetly observe and score the team's performance as well as help administer the test. If a trainer is not available, then any person can act as the assistant and record the entire test on video.

Additional Exercises: You may include additional exercises in this test to further demonstrate the extent of your dog's training after completing required exercises.

Scoring: The team must receive a minimum score of 200 out of 250 to pass, and the team must receive either a 4 or 5 on every exercise.

Live Alerts: If the dog alerts to an unplanned, medical event during this test, usual alert protocol should be followed and the rest of the test can be continued. The camera should continue recording throughout the process but the results of the alert and occurrences throughout will not be considered when determining if the team passed.

General Requirements: Throughout the test the dog must be calm and confident without becoming overly focused on its environment.

When walking with the handler, the dog should be in heel position unless commanded otherwise. Heel position is defined as: remaining within 1 foot of the handler in all directions, maintaining a loose leash, no forging or lagging, changing speed with the handler, turning corners promptly, and halting when the handler stops. The dog may remain on either side of the handler and the handler may talk to the dog and reward when necessary.

Public Access Testing

Exercise Descriptions

The 20 exercises below are ordered to naturally flow. If you need to complete the test in another order, it is permitted as long as every exercise is clearly demonstrated.

1. **Exiting The Vehicle**
The handler will exit the car, prepare the dog as needed, then release the dog from the car.

Expectations: The dog remains in the car until released verbally, then exits the car and patiently remains next to the handler in a safe position. The dog responds to commands and the handler provides the necessary cues to keep the dog under control and in a safe position at all times.

2. **Approaching & Entering A Store**
The team will walk across the parking lot, toward the store, and then enter the store.

Expectations: The dog is in heel position and shows no significant reaction toward traffic or distractions. When entering the store, the handler is able to manipulate the doors in a manner that keeps the dog safe and under control.

3. **Heeling Through A Store**
After entering through the doors, the team will walk through the store for a minimum of 1 minute. (While this exercise lasts for 1 minute, heeling will be evaluated and considered throughout the entire test.)

Expectations: The dog is in heel position at all times and is not distracted by the environment and does not attempt to solicit attention.

4. **Startle Recovery**
While heeling through the store, the assistant will drop a clipboard within 5 feet of the dog. The handler may remain neutral or may respond with praise to counteract a potentially negative event.

Expectations: The dog continues heeling next to the handler after the event. (The dog is permitted to startle, jump, or turn, but may not demonstrate any aggression or prolonged fear.) The handler either does not respond to the event or interacts with the dog in a kind and positive manner.

5. **Ascending/Descending In A Building**
The team will move to a different level of the store (up or down 1 floor), and then return. The team may demonstrate any method which they frequently use - stairs, elevator, ramp, or escalator. (Please be aware of the risks an escalator poses for dogs and that it is rarely necessary to train a dog to utilize them. However, if it is necessary for your team and you wish to demonstrate it, that is acceptable if done safely).

Expectations: The dog remains in heel position and is calm and confident throughout. The dog does not interact with the environment or people in the vicinity. The handler ensures the dog's safety at all times (e.g. ensuring the dog's tail is far from the elevator doors).

6. **Heeling With A Cart**
The team will begin walking while the handler pushes a cart, as if shopping in a store. At minimum they should demonstrate: walking, stopping, a left turn, and a right turn. This should last

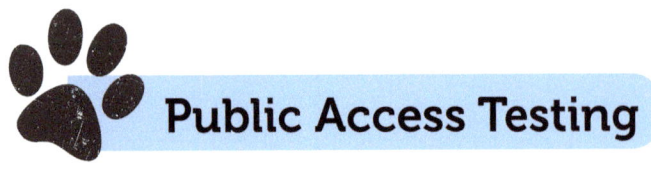

Public Access Testing

long enough to demonstrate the dog's proficiency.

Expectations: The dog remains in heel position, or a slightly altered heel position which continues to keep the dog safe and out of the public's way. The dog is calm and confident, does not shy away from the cart, does not interact with merchandise, halts when the handler stops, and turns corners promptly without straying from the handler and cart.

7. Purchasing Food

The team will enter a food court or eating establishment and order food at a counter.

Expectations: The dog remains in heel position until the handler reaches the counter. At the counter the dog either remains in heel position, moves to a position between the handler and the counter, or is positioned in another manner which is unobtrusive. The dog remains calm and does not solicit attention or attempt to sniff or lick any surface. The handler maintains control over the dog and is able to focus on ordering without needing to constantly provide the dog with commands and guidance.

(Note: Food courts are excellent locations for this exercise as you order at a counter and then can easily demonstrate the next exercises.)

8. Carrying a Plate or Tray of Food

The handler will carry a plate or tray of food while the dog is heeling. The handler may talk to the dog as much as necessary.

Expectations: The dog remains focused and in heel position without soliciting attention or attempting to sniff or lick any surface. The dog's behavior allows the handler to safely and effectively carry the items.

9. Restaurant

The handler will approach a seat in a restaurant or eating establishment. The handler will direct the dog to go under their table or chair until finished with the meal.

Expectations. The dog approaches the table calmly and confidently and follows the handler's cues to lay under the table or chair. The handler directs the dog to lay in a manner which is safe for the dog and out of the public's footpath. The dog remains relaxed throughout the meal; it may move slightly for comfort but should not be up and down or need repeated instructions. The dog does not solicit attention or attempt to eat anything or lick any surface.

10. Medical Alert in Public

At some point during the restaurant exercise, the handler will open a scent sample which the dog has been trained to alert to *(i.e. a low blood sugar sample)*. The sample will be opened and/or rubbed on the handler's skin in a manner that does not allow the dog to hear or see it. The sample will be within 6 feet of the dog for the entirety of the time it is exposed. The handler will then wait until the dog alerts, for a maximum of 5 minutes, without giving any other cues. When the dog alerts correctly, the handler will respond and reward as appropriate.

Expectations: The dog alerts within 5 minutes in a calm and professional manner without becoming disruptive or hyperactive. The handler rewards the dog in a positive manner which encourages the behavior but is not disruptive to those around them.

11. Resisting Dropped Food

At some point during the restaurant

Public Access Testing

exercise, the handler will drop at least one piece of food on the floor within 1 foot of the dog. The handler may give additional verbal commands to instruct the dog to leave the food. The food should be left for a minimum of 15 seconds before being picked up.

Expectations: The dog does not eat, lick, or sniff the food, and remains in the down position. The handler picks the food up from the floor and does not allow the dog to eat the food from the floor at any point.

(Note: the next exercise requires food as well. It may be helpful to pick the food up from the floor, but keep it for the next exercise)

12. Basic Obedience Next to Food

After exiting the restaurant or eating establishment, a plate or pile of food will be placed on the ground. The team will then walk in a straight line directly past the food, passing the food within approximately 2 feet. The team will then turn around and approach the food again, but when the food is next to the dog (within 2 feet), the handler will stop and ask the dog for a sit; when the dog obeys the team will then continue walking past the food. The team will turn around and approach the food for the third time. When the food is next to the dog (within 2 feet), the handler will stop and ask the dog for a down; when the dog complies the team will then continue walking past.

Expectations: The dog obeys commands promptly and does not attempt to eat, sniff, or lick the food. The handler is not harsh and is able to maintain control of the dog while next to the food distraction. After the exercise is completed the handler or assistant picks up the food and any mess that was made.

13. Dropped Lead

At some point during the test, the handler will drop the lead on the ground while continuing to walk a minimum of 20 feet before holding the lead again.

Expectations: The dog remains under control and in heel position. The handler is able to maintain control of the dog at all times and retrieve the lead again.

14. Recall to Heel

The handler will place the dog in a sit or down position and cue them to stay. The handler will then walk at least 6 feet directly away from the dog and stop. The handler will then either call the dog into heel position, or turn to face the dog and call the dog to their front. The handler will then retrieve the lead if needed and continue walking with the dog in a heel position.

Expectations: The dog remains in the sit or down stay until called. The dog comes promptly and directly to the handler showing no hesitation and without soliciting attention or being distracted by the environment. The team begins walking forward smoothly after the recall.

15. Down Stay

The handler will place the dog in a down stay and, while continuing to hold the lead, will walk in a circle around the dog 3 times.

Expectations: The dog promptly moves into the down position and remains in position until released.

16. Handler Greeting Stranger

From a heel position, the handler will

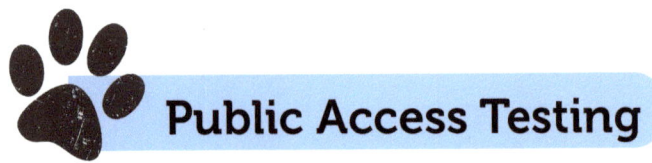

Public Access Testing

greet a stranger with a handshake or equivalent. The stranger should be instructed to ask to pet the dog, and the handler will politely yet confidently deny.

Expectations: The dog remains calm and confident, and does not attempt to interact with the person. The handler is able to confidently and politely communicate that the dog is working and may not be pet.

17. Person Petting From Behind

With the dog in a heel position, a stranger (can be the same person as Exercise 16), will approach from behind and pet the dog's back for approximately 5 seconds before walking away. The handler may use verbal commands to keep the dog in heel position.

Expectations: The dog remains in heel position and remains focused on the handler. The dog does not show any fear or aggression, or become overly excited. The handler is able to maintain the dog's focus in a positive manner.

18. Exiting Store & Approaching Vehicle

The team will exit the store's doors and walk across the parking lot, toward the vehicle.

Expectations: When exiting the store, the handler is able to manipulate the doors in a manner that keeps the dog safe and under control, and the dog remains calm and confident. The dog is in heel position and shows no significant reaction toward traffic or distractions.

19. Entering The Vehicle

The handler will approach the vehicle and prepare the dog and vehicle as needed. The handler will then cue the dog to enter the car. If the dog is too small to enter the vehicle independently, it may be placed in the vehicle by the handler.

Expectations: The dog patiently waits outside the vehicle until cued to enter. The handler prepares the dog and the vehicle as necessary to keep the dog safe and maintains control of the dog throughout. The dog does not demonstrate avoidance or hesitancy when entering.

20. Dog & Handler Relationship

At all points during the test the dog and handler should demonstrate a positive relationship without stress or hesitation from either individual. The handler should provide occasional positive reinforcement at appropriate times and the dog should remain focused on the handler or on performing its tasks with no or occasional food rewards. The dog should be as inconspicuous as possible and the team should positively represent service dogs at all times to everyone around them.

Public Access Testing

MD Dogs Public Access Test

DOG NAME: _____

DOG BREED: _____

DOG D.O.B.: _____

HANDLER NAME: _____

EVALUATOR NAME: _____

EVALUATOR CREDENTIALS (IF ANY):
_____

DATE OF TEST: _____

LOCATION OF TEST:
_____

EQUIPMENT USED:
_____
_____
_____

FINAL RESULT (PLEASE CIRCLE ONE):   PASS   FAIL

NOTES: _____

_____

_____

_____

_____

_____

_____

_____

_____

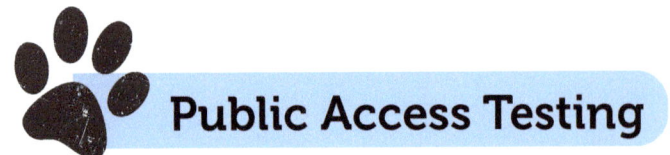

Public Access Testing

✓ 1 = Very Poor
✓ 2 = Poor
✓ 3 = Fair
✓ 4 = Good
✓ 5 = Excellent

1. Exiting the Vehicle The dog remained in the car until released and then waited patiently outside vehicle without pulling on leash. The handler maintained safe control of the dog.	1 2 3 4 5 1 2 3 4 5
2. Approaching & Entering A Store The dog maintained heel position and showed no significant reaction toward traffic or distractions. The handler manipulated the doors to keep the dog safe and under control.	1 2 3 4 5 1 2 3 4 5
3. Heeling Through A Store The dog was in heel position at all times (refer to the definition outlined at the beginning of the test) The dog was not distracted by the environment and did not attempt to solicit attention.	1 2 3 4 5 1 2 3 4 5
4. Startle Recovery The dog did not demonstrate any aggression or prolonged fear. The dog continued heeling next to the handler after the event. The handler either did not respond to the event or interacted with the dog in a kind and positive manner.	1 2 3 4 5 1 2 3 4 5 1 2 3 4 5
5. Ascending/Descending In A Building The dog remained in heel position and did not interact with the environment or people in the vicinity. The dog was calm and confident throughout. The handler ensured the dog's safety at all times.	1 2 3 4 5 1 2 3 4 5 1 2 3 4 5
6. Heeling with a Cart The dog remained in heel position, or a slightly altered heel position which continued to keep the dog safe and out of the public's way. The dog was calm and confident; did not shy away from the cart. The dog did not interact with merchandise.	1 2 3 4 5 1 2 3 4 5 1 2 3 4 5

✓ 1 = Very Poor
✓ 2 = Poor
✓ 3 = Fair
✓ 4 = Good
✓ 5 = Excellent

Public Access Testing

7. Purchasing Food At the counter the dog remained in heel position, moved to a position between the handler and the counter, or was positioned in another manner which was unobtrusive. The dog remained calm and did not solicit attention or attempt to sniff or lick any surface. The handler maintained control over the dog and was able to focus on ordering without needing to constantly provide the dog with commands or guidance.	1 2 3 4 5 1 2 3 4 5 1 2 3 4 5
8. Carrying a Plate or Tray of Food The dog remained focused and in heel position without soliciting attention or attempting to sniff or lick any surface. The dog's behavior allowed the handler to safely and effectively carry the items.	1 2 3 4 5 1 2 3 4 5
9. Restaurant The dog followed the handler's cues to lay under the table or chair. The handler directed the dog to lay in a manner which was safe for the dog and out of the public's footpath. The dog remained relaxed throughout the meal and did not solicit attention or attempt to eat anything or lick any surface.	1 2 3 4 5 1 2 3 4 5 1 2 3 4 5
10. Medical Alert in Public The dog alerted within 5 minutes in a calm and professional manner without becoming disruptive or hyperactive. The handler rewarded the dog in a positive manner which encouraged the behavior but was not disruptive to those around them.	1 2 3 4 5 1 2 3 4 5
11. Resisting Dropped Food The dog did not eat, lick, or sniff the food, and remained in the down position. The handler picked the food up from the floor and did not allow the dog to eat the food from the floor at any point.	1 2 3 4 5 1 2 3 4 5

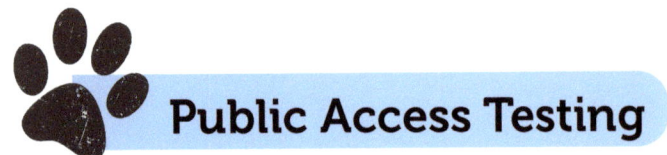
Public Access Testing

✓ 1 = Very Poor
✓ 2 = Poor
✓ 3 = Fair
✓ 4 = Good
✓ 5 = Excellent

12. Basic Obedience Next to Food	
The dog obeyed commands promptly and did not attempt to eat, sniff, or lick the food.	1 2 3 4 5
The handler was not harsh and was able to maintain control of the dog while next to the food distraction.	1 2 3 4 5
13. Dropped Lead	
The dog remained under control and in heel position.	1 2 3 4 5
The handler was able to retrieve the lead and maintain control of the dog at all times.	1 2 3 4 5
14. Recall to Heel	
The dog remained in the sit or down stay.	1 2 3 4 5
The dog came promptly and directly to the handler, showing no hesitation and without soliciting attention or being distracted.	1 2 3 4 5
The team easily transitioned into a heel after the recall.	1 2 3 4 5
15. Down Stay	
The dog promptly moved into the down position.	1 2 3 4 5
The dog remained in position until released.	1 2 3 4 5
16. Handler Greeting Stranger	
The dog remained calm and confident, and did not attempt to interact with the person.	1 2 3 4 5
The handler was able to confidently and politely communicate that the dog is working and may not be pet.	1 2 3 4 5
17. Person Petting From Behind	
The dog remained in heel position and remained focused on the handler.	1 2 3 4 5
The dog did not show any fear or aggression, or become overly excited.	1 2 3 4 5
The handler was able to maintain the dog's focus in a positive manner.	1 2 3 4 5

✓ 1 = Very Poor
✓ 2 = Poor
✓ 3 = Fair
✓ 4 = Good
✓ 5 = Excellent

Public Access Testing

18. Exiting Store & Approaching Vehicle The handler manipulated the doors to keep the dog safe and under control.	1 2 3 4 5
The dog maintained heel position and showed no significant reaction towards traffic or distractions.	1 2 3 4 5
19. Entering The Vehicle The handler prepared the dog and the vehicle as necessary to keep the dog safe, and maintained control of the dog throughout.	1 2 3 4 5
The dog patiently waited outside the vehicle until cued to enter and did not demonstrate avoidance or hesitancy when entering.	1 2 3 4 5
20. Dog & Handler Relationship The dog and handler demonstrated a positive relationship and the handler provided occasional positive reinforcement at appropriate times.	1 2 3 4 5
The dog was able to work for occasional or no treats.	1 2 3 4 5
The dog remained focused on the handler or on performing its tasks and was relaxed, confident, and friendly.	1 2 3 4 5
The handler managed the dog to ensure its behavior was as inconspicuous as possible and the team positively represented Service Dogs at all times to everyone around them.	1 2 3 4 5
The handler treated the business and customers with respect regarding the service dog.	1 2 3 4 5

Copyrighted Information

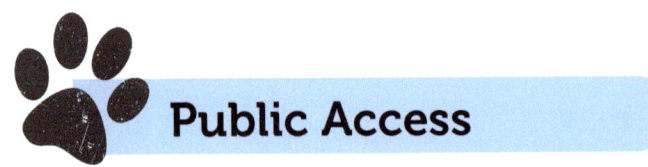

Public Access

Flying with your Service Dog
(in the United States)

Flying with a service dog for the first time can be nerve wracking! There are many aspects to consider and it takes a lot of preparation. But with a properly trained dog and some preparation it will be smooth sailing...or flying.

PACKING LIST

- ☐ Travel bowl
- ☐ Empty water bottle (can fill up after security)
- ☐ 1 serving of food (in case luggage doesn't arrive on time)
- ☐ Place blanket (the floor of the plane gets very cold)
- ☐ Toy (to occupy her if necessary)
- ☐ Pick up bags
- ☐ Wipes (in case anything needs cleaning – best to be prepared!)
- ☐ Leash
- ☐ Collar
- ☐ Vest
- ☐ Documentation required by your airline

Preparation

Practice having your DAD lie down in small spaces for long periods of time, such as the floorboard of your car. This will help prepare her for lying underneath the seat in front of you on the flight.

48 hours before your flight call the airline to inform them that you have a service dog with you. Read the airline's requirements for service dogs - some require a vest or other identification to be on the dog. Keep in mind that airlines are not required to follow the ADA, instead they follow the ACAA (Air Carrier Access Act). Because of this, they are not required to accept service dogs in training and health records and TSA documentation can be required. The ACAA is changing regularly and in 2020 major changes were presented, eliminating the transportation of Emotional Support Dogs and permitting addition records to be required. For more details about the laws regarding air travel, read the Department of Transportation's ruling regarding the ACAA - found at www.transportation.gov.

Once you have booked your flight, you may request bulkhead seating if you'd like, however I have found that my dogs are often more comfortable in regular seating. You are not required to pay a pet fee because your dog is a service dog, however you may not request an extra seat if your dog is too large, you would have to purchase another ticket.

Limit your dog's food and water intake 12 hours before.

Prior to leaving for the airport, exercise

Public Access

her to get any energy out.

Before you go through security, make sure that you take your dog outside to relieve herself one last time.

Security

When going through security, you are not required to take off your DAD's gear. However if your dog keeps the gear on and causes the metal detector to sound, then a TSA agent will pat her down. I find that this is distracting for the dogs and takes a bit of time. Instead, I prefer to take all, or almost all, my dog's gear off.

I remove my dog's gear (vest, collar, leash, etc.) and have her heel with a metal free leash as as I move my belongings up to the x-ray machine. When it is our turn, I put my dog in a sit stay then I walk through the detector. As long as it does not sound then I call my dog through the detector. I then ask her to heel as we walk to have my hands swabbed (this is required for service dog teams). She stays in a sit by my side while my hands are swabbed and when we are finished she heels with me to gather my belongings and I put her gear back on.

As you walk through the airport, be particularly mindful of luggage that is hanging off of someone's shoulder that may bump into your dog, or bags that are being rolled behind someone. Travelers are particularly unaware as they are often stressed and in a rush, so be sure to be the one to watch out for your dog's safety. Also watch out for the pets and emotional support dogs in airports that have not been properly trained.

On the plane

At the gate you may ask to pre-board which can help because you can get seated and have your DAD get situated without being rushed by others behind you or squeezing by the other people in your row.

If there is a passenger next to you, always ask them if they are afraid of or allergic to dogs. I have never had a problem, but it is a courtesy to check with them and if there is a problem they can request a seat change.

Take off and landing are the most stressful parts of flying, as the dogs don't understand what is going on. Remind her to stay and quietly and calmly praise her throughout to let her know she's okay.

During the flight it's best to not have your dog chew on a toy, but if it's needed to keep her calm then it's better than having her be restless and draw attention. Try to choose something that is quiet – not a loud bone that she will be gnawing on. While airplanes are loud, the goal is still to have your dog be invisible.

Public Access

I have had dogs that sleep through entire flights, but I've also had dogs that sleep then suddenly pop up as if they are in pain. We aren't entirely sure of the effects of air pressure changes, but it is possible some dogs are affected by it or specific sounds we do not recognize. If your dog jumps up or seems to be in pain suddenly, rub her ears and praise her until she is relaxed and returns to a down.

When leaving the plane, it's much easier to wait until most passengers have left. This lets you avoid the rush of people trying to get to their next flight who may not see your dog and injure her. If you need to get somewhere quickly, then just be aware of your dog's position at all times and do your best to keep others from stepping or bumping into her.

After you de-plane, before you pick up your luggage it's best to take your dog outside to relieve herself. Usually there are a few minutes of waiting before the luggage is unloaded, so it's not a rush and this will give your dog relief and you relief knowing she won't have an accident inside!

Remember to be prepared, be educated regarding the most recent laws, and be relaxed so your dog is too!

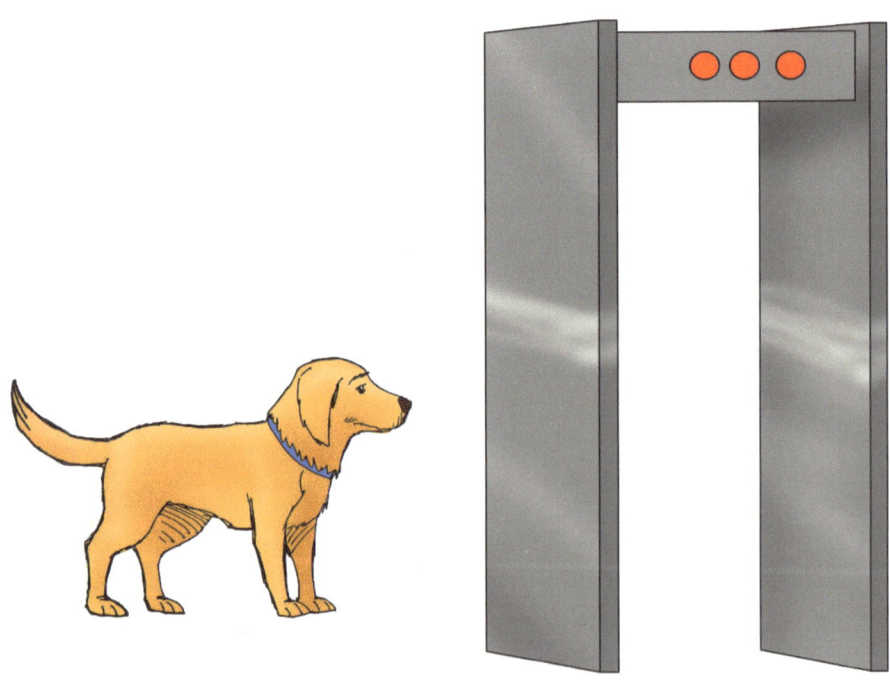

Public Access

Going to School with Your Service Dog

Below are tips about going to school with a service dog. These are not all necessary, however they are suggestions for how to make it go smoothly.

- First contact the disability office at your school or your instructors, to request an accommodation so you are able to bring your service dog. If your dog is still in training, look into your state laws to determine if in training dogs are given access rights with self-training handlers.

- If the dog is for a young child who is not able to handle the dog yet, the school is not required to provide a handler for the dog. Because of this, sometimes it's better to have the dog stay at home during the day until the child is old enough to handle the dog.

- Only take your dog when you are absolutely sure she can lie down and be completely silent for the length of your class. If for any reason the dog becomes disruptive, immediately remove her from the classroom. The class should never suffer because of your service dog.

- To introduce your DAD to attending class, start by bringing her to just one class each day. Then gradually add in additional classes when you see that she is succeeding.

- If the classroom floors are hard and do not have carpet, a place blanket can make her more comfortable and less restless because hard floors can be cold and difficult on their joints.

- Do not allow people to pet the dog, otherwise you will never get anywhere!

- Before your first classes, visit the classrooms to determine how to best prepare for class as well as where your dog will be placed. Certain chairs are particularly difficult to fit a dog under, so

Public Access

you may need to sit next to a wall or other barrier to keep her out of the way. Additionally, find locations nearest to the building where you can take her to relieve herself before and after each class, as well as the nearest trash cans.

- Sitting in the same seat or same general area is considerate to others. This allows someone who is allergic or who has a fear of dogs to intentionally sit furthest from you without being confrontational or causing a disruption.

- Going to school can be incredibly stressful for a dog – there are people everywhere, students may be rushing to another class and bump into her or step on her tail, there are bags hanging that sometimes bump into her, doors are being opened towards her, potentially squishing her paws, food is often eaten around her, and on top of all this the handler is asking the dog to be on her best behavior and perform her tasks. Because of this it is incredibly important to pay close attention to your dog's body language while at school. I want my dog's tail to be up, for her to be happy, and to be focused. Of course as she goes throughout the day she may get tired and that's okay, but I pay attention to that and make sure the experience is positive. If she looks like she is stressed, give her more treats and praise, and possibly a break. Then when you get home evaluate the situation to determine if perhaps she should only attend shorter periods of school or even not attend. Not every dog is capable of attending school with you.

- A school day is often incredibly long. Make sure to give her breaks throughout the day. I always let my dogs have a lunch break – when I eat lunch I sit outside when possible and take off her vest to play tug or fetch. Even if it's just for 3-5 minutes, it will let her brain have a break and prevent her from dreading school (I wish this worked for me too!).

Public Access

- It is the handler's job to protect the dog. Sometimes, especially in middle school and high school, students may bark at the dog, pull her tail, etc. You must pay attention to your surroundings and the second you notice this, stand up for your dog. Even if you are a non-confrontational person, not addressing these behaviors is the fastest way to have your dog hate going to school and become afraid of crowded areas. This will cause your dog to fail as a DAD, even after all the training you have put into her.

- When you are in class and your DAD alerts, verify the alert and if she is correct, have a puppy party. But puppy parties should be much different than your puppy parties at home. Give high value treats and petting behind the ears, but don't be overly active and don't verbally praise her unless you leave the room. Soft, high value treats are best so that the chewing won't be too loud to distract others. It's important to balance the training of your DAD with respect for those around you as even after

an alert, the goal is for your dog to be inconspicuous.

- The majority of classes are appropriate for a DAD to attend. However, if you are enrolled in a laboratory that will involve harsh chemicals, dangerous conditions, little space, or overwhelming scents, you may want to leave your DAD at home for her safety. Discuss this with your teacher, professor or disability office to determine the best situation to keep both you and your DAD safe.

- If your DAD attends school with you during day, she will need a long nap in the afternoon if you want to try to teach her to alert at night. Dogs need a lot of sleep and attending school is exhausting.

Public Access

Going to Work with Your Service Dog

Because the workplace is not considered a place of public access, the protocol surrounding service dogs is different.

Title 1 of the Americans With Disabilities Act (See "Resources" to read more about it and other laws regarding service dogs) details employment provisions. However, under title 1 there is no definition for a service animal and it does not give guidelines for employers to follow. As a result, an employee must request a reasonable accommodation to have a service animal and it should be processed the same as any other reasonable accommodation request. The reasonable accommodation is the request to have an exception to a typical no pets policy. An employee may request to have a service dog, service dog in training, or even an emotional support animal in order to meet the individual's need. However, the workplace may request documentation, make suggestions, and does not have to accept the request. If there is not a no pets policy in place and other employees bring pets into the workplace, then a reasonable accommodation request is not required.

In general, employers should provide this accommodation. However, the ADA does allow employers to choose

among effective accommodations, so technically an employer may choose a different type of solution. However, especially for a task such as diabetic alert, another solution is not a possibility so a reasonable accommodation should usually be made. But for a handler requesting this accommodation, this means that you should explain the task the dog does in order to show that another accommodation is not possible.

Unlike public accommodations, employers do have the right to ask for documentation regarding the service animal. This means they are permitted to ask for a doctor's note, trainer's note, or if the dog was self-trained for a demonstration that the dog is capable of handling a work place environment.

It's important to know the laws prior to requesting your service dog accompany you to work, but remain respectful and patient if you need to educate your employer about the laws. Remember that the workplace is not a place of public access, so the laws regarding it are different and your employer has the right to ask for proof, documentation, etc.

Public Access

"Graduating" your Diabetic Alert Dog

There are two parts to a fully trained DAD – sufficient public access training and sufficient scent training. To demonstrate sufficient public access skills, complete the Public Access Test. No dog will be perfect 100% of the time, but a fully public access trained service dog should be perfect about 95% of the time. This means no sniffing, no soliciting attention, always focused on her handler, etc.

To demonstrate sufficient scent training, keep a log of your dog's alerts. When your dog is correctly live alerting with a success of at least 70% for 5 weeks, then you know her live alerting is quite accurate. But for an even clearer picture of her understanding, perform a double blind scent wheel test with 1 low sample and 2 in-range samples. If she correctly indicates with 90% success it's clear she has a thorough understanding! (Video this exercise and store it for record keeping!)

While not legally required, it is safe to consider your DAD fully trained when your dog:

1) Has passed the public access test

2) Is live alerting correctly 70% of the time

3) And can perform at 90% success on a double blind scent wheel test.

MD Dogs Inc offers a voluntary verification process if you would like to ensure that your dog is trained to MD Dogs standards specifically. The verification process requires alert logs and videos of particular scent training exercises, as well as the MD Dogs Public Access Test. When a team passes MD Dogs Verification, they receive MD Dogs branded materials, become a part of the MD Dogs Verified teams community, and may contact MD Dogs for assistance demonstrating proof of their dog's training (i.e. if a school is requesting additional proof). This process is completely voluntary and is **not** required to have a fully trained Diabetic Alert Dog; Verification is only required to be formally associated with MD Dogs as a tool for you, to provide clarity that your dog is fully trained to MD Dogs standards. For more information visit MDdogs.org.

Public Access

Washing Out A Diabetic Alert Dog in Training

A "wash out" is a dog that is determined to not be suitable as a public access service dog any longer. Many dogs are not capable of being a service dog, it is hard work and takes an intelligent, driven, and yet people pleasing dog. Always talk to a professional trainer prior to making the decision to wash out your DAD in training, as some behaviors can be fixed with the right approach. If the behaviors continue, but the dog successfully alerts to out-of-range blood sugar levels, you can continue scent training so she can be an in-home service dog.

Below are a few reasons why a DAD in training might wash out.

Human Aggression or Protection

If a dog shows any aggression – at home or elsewhere – stop all public access training and visit a trainer. Aggression involves growling, snapping, or biting a person for any reason. A service dog must be able to handle difficult situations without demonstrating aggression. If a child comes up to your dog unknowingly and pulls her ears, tail, gets in her face, or sends all the wrong signals to the dog, a service dog still must tolerate it or avoid the situation some other way. But aggression should never be the way the dog handles the situation. This is because we cannot predict everything that happens in public, and the public may not be put at risk.

Service dogs also cannot be protective of their handler. If your dog shows signs of being protective, consult a service dog trainer quickly and pause all public access training. If an emergency situation were to occur and a medical team could not get to you because your dog was protecting you, it could be dangerous for both you and your dog. Signals of protection are showing aggressive behaviors (above) while routinely placing herself between a person approaching you or people coming into contact with you.

Even if your dog is not considered 'dangerous' (i.e. you don't think she would ever hurt someone), if your dog shows any of these behaviors she is still not suitable for service work. But she may still be a wonderful at home Diabetic Alert Dog or pet.

Public Access

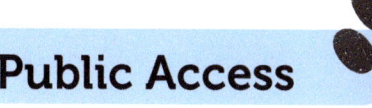

Anxiety

Some dogs, especially those who were not socialized as puppies, become anxious or fearful adults. This can be demonstrated a few ways:

1. Startling and not recovering quickly

2. Demonstrating stress signals when in public (scratching, panting, lip licking, yawning, stretching)

3. Being hyper-aware

4. Being unable to relax when in public.

While these behaviors are not dangerous, if the dog cannot overcome her anxiety then she may not be able to focus on her handler's glucose levels and alert properly.

Dog Reactivity

Dog reactivity is demonstrated by barking, lunging, or growling at other dogs. While a DAD may not typically see other dogs in public, if there ever is another service dog and your DAD disrupts it by being reactive, it could cause that service dog to miss an alert, misguide its handler, etc. It is not fair to put other handlers in danger because of your dog's behavior, no matter how infrequently you think you will see another service dog. Additionally, if your dog cannot properly behave around other dogs, this negatively reflects upon all service dogs.

Personality

Dogs have different personalities just like people. Some dogs may not enjoy being a service dog and that doesn't mean as a trainer you have failed. I suggest performing temperament tests on all potential DADs. Also begin training when your pup is 8 weeks old and always keep public access fun and exciting for your puppy. This will all help maximize the chance that your dog will thrive as a working dog.

If your dog begins to not want to go to work - has a dropped tail and ears back while in public, does not perform commands quickly, or just seems unhappy when working - take a step back from public access training. Do training at home for a bit, make sure the vest fits properly or try a different vest style (sometimes dogs get vest

Public Access

aversion), and retrain the basics. Incorporate fun training games, then try public access again. If she seemed to enjoy staying home more than accompanying you in public, it may be a sign that she'd prefer to be your pet rather than your service dog.

Medical Reasons

Hip dysplasia is a very common reason to wash out a service dog or retire her. Public access training is difficult on a dog's body. They are constantly walking, getting up, laying on hard floors, slipping, etc. If your dog has hip dysplasia it will be painful for your dog to accompany you in public. A dog with hip dysplasia may be able to work at home as a DAD, but it would not be humane to ask a dog to work in public with such a condition.

Any other medical issue that would cause the dog to be in pain when in public would automatically result in the dog being washed out. It is important to keep in mind that the dog's purpose in public is to take care of its handler. If the dog has a medical condition that prevents her from being able to focus, causes decreased abilities, or causes pain, the dog cannot do its job any longer and should not work in public as a service dog. Remember that our dogs are supposed to watch over us, but we have to do our part and watch over them too.

Acknowledgements

M.D. Dogs Inc
Diabetic Alert Dog Training Steps

Acknowledgements

Acknowledgements

It is only through the support and encouragement of numerous individuals that this book became a reality. I am so appreciative to those who guided, educated, and helped along the way, allowing me to share my knowledge with others through both MD Dogs Inc. and *Diabetic Alert Dog Training Steps.*

Thank you to all those who have taught me. The field of Diabetic Alert Dogs is relatively young and scientifically quite unknown, but the PennVet Working Dog Center, speakers at the PennVet Working Dog Conferences and AKC Scent Detection Conference, and Debby Kay are all working to move the field forward and have been instrumental in my understanding of these dogs and their training. Additionally, thank you to the University Scholars Program at Penn for providing funding to attend workshops, and providing me with the unique opportunity and inspiration to combine dog training with academia.

To Isaac from Ibis Lagumbay Art, Jeannie Francis, and Laura Reynolds - thank you for demonstrating such patience with my requests and modifications for illustrations, photos, and layouts. You all are the reason I can be proud of this book, and you have provided its professional and crisp appearance that I could never have accomplished on my own.

To those who planted this idea many years ago - Caleb Long and his family, Kathy Burgess, and the McCarty family - thank you for your faith in me, for your big ideas, and for your encouragement. Your suggestions and never-ending optimism, provided me the initiative to attempt to train a Diabetic Alert Dog and enter this field that I am now so passionate about.

To Scott Smith - you would certainly fit in the "education" category, but your involvement and assistance was so much more than that. You took seriously the 16-year-old who showed up at your conference, with her mom beside her, claiming that she was going to try to train a Diabetic Alert Dog from the litter of puppies that she was raising in her bathroom. In a field where trainers are so quick to judge, cut down, and dismiss newcomers, you not only educated, but you encouraged and supported me. And when I was at a crossroads, significantly uncertain, you picked up the phone and provided clear guidance that shaped

Acknowledgements

the way I thought about Diabetic Alert Dogs. Thank you for your sincerity and kindness that enabled me to grow and serve others.

Lastly, thank you to the six who have taught me more than anyone - Mackenzie, Annie, Kylee, Maggie, Emily, and Bri. You have taught me about diabetes, persistence, acceptance, and selflessness. Each of you are incredible individuals who have the remarkable tenacity and strength to fight this exhausting, terrifying disease 24 hours a day, yet the kindness and patience to still care for those around you and even welcome me into your families. You are the reason I have such a passion for training these dogs. Each one of you has impacted me more than words can ever say. Thank you for letting me be a part of your story.

Resources

Resources

**M.D. Dogs Inc
Diabetic Alert Dog Training Steps**

Resources

Resources

Financial Estimate for Training a Diabetic Alert Dog

Self training a Diabetic Alert Dog will most likely be less expensive than purchasing a fully trained dog, as you will not be paying for the trainer's time. But, training your own DAD is still not cheap. Below is an estimate for the cost to train your own DAD from a 2 month old puppy until it is 9 months old (The majority of expenses occur in these first months). You can save money by perhaps purchasing a used crate or toys, and not using a Kuranda cot. However, I do not recommend trying to save money when it comes to two things - the purchase of the puppy and the private lessons with a service dog trainer. Buying an inexpensive puppy from someone who has not done health testing on the parents could result in the pup having medical issues, especially a genetic condition (hip dysplasia, heart defect, etc.) that will prevent her from becoming a working service dog or that requires her to retire early. From a financial standpoint, it is worth it to invest in a healthy dog that will have a working life of 8-10 years rather than to save a few hundred dollars to purchase a dog that will have a shorter working life. Additionally, having an experienced trainer available to give suggestions and answer questions will greatly increase your likelihood of success.

$100 - $2,500	Purchase of dog
$500	Test strips (You will be testing more frequently)
$300	Veterinarian visits, shots, flea medicine, etc.
$300-$600	Evaluations of hips and elbows (PennHIP and/or OFA)
$250	Alerting rewards (raw dog food, meat, etc.)
$160	Dog food
$300	Kuranda cot, crate, toys, chews
$200	Service vests, boots, coats, and other supplies.
$400-$1,000	Private lessons with a service dog trainer.

Total: $2,510 to $5,810

United States Service Dog Laws

AMERICANS WITH DISABILITIES ACT (ADA) – Public Access

The Americans with Disabilities Act is the primary law governing service dogs. Read more about it online and know the laws like the back of your hand.

STATE LAWS – Public Access

The Americans with Disabilities Act does not cover service dogs in training. This is determined by each state. Many states give service dogs in training the same access rights as fully trained service dogs, but not all. Additionally, some states only give access rights to service dog trainers rather than owners who are currently training a service dog. If your state does not give access to service dogs in training, then it is still possible to train a DAD, but public access training will have to be more intentional. All public access trips should be in pet friendly stores. When your dog is able to pass the Public Access Test, showing she is qualified to be a fully trained service dog, then you can replace her "in training" patches with "Service Dog" patches and begin taking her to non pet friendly stores. This will take more time and effort, but it is important to respect the laws in your state, regardless.

FAIR HOUSING ACT - Housing

The resident must submit a reasonable accommodation request, stating that they would like to have a service animal. This essentially states that if the resident or potential resident has a disability and the animal is trained to mitigate the disability, then a no pets policy does not apply to the individual and their animal. There are a few exceptions, so read the Fair Housing Act if living or requesting to live in a location that does not allow pets.

AIR CARRIER ACCESS ACT – Air Travel

In 2020, the Department of Transportation released a new ruling which does not require airlines to accept Emotional Support Animals on flights, and which permits airlines to require service dog health records and a TSA form to be provided at least 48 hours prior to flying. A doctor's note is not required. However the dog must be able to fit at your feet or on your lap in order to be permitted. For the most up to date requirements, visit www.transportation.gov.

*Laws are always changing so be sure to research them thoroughly for yourself prior to beginning training

M.D. Dogs Inc
Diabetic Alert Dog Training Steps
Records

Records

Exposure List

This is not an exhaustive list, but can be used as a guideline. Check off the things your puppy experiences to keep track. It is recommended that your pup is exposed to each of these items between 8-12 weeks and again between 3-9 months to solidify the experience.

	8-12 Weeks	3–9 months
Animals		
Birds		
Cats		
Cows		
Ducks		
Horses		
Large dogs (male)		
Large dogs (female)		
Puppies		
Small dogs (male)		
Small dogs (female)		
Squirrels		
Handling		
Brushing fur		
Brushing teeth		
Checking between pads		
Checking teeth		
Cleaning ears		
Clipping nails		
Grasping muzzle		
Holding puppy		
Hugging puppy		
Touching belly		
Touching collar		
Touching ears		
Touching paws		
Touching rear legs		
Touching tail		
Locations		
Veterinarian		
Park		

	8-12 Weeks	3–9 months
Noise & Visual		
Airplanes		
Alarms		
Balloons		
Banging on pots/pans		
Bicycles		
Brooms		
Busses		
Cars		
Crowds		
Crutches		
Doorbell		
Dropping item >4ft		
Dropping item <4ft		
Fairs/Festivals		
Fireworks		
Garbage bag		
Garbage can		
Gym equipment		
Helicopter		
Honking		
Indoor shopping mall		
Inflated object		
Jack hammer		
Knocking on doors		
Loud radios		
Motorcycles		
Rollerblades		
Shopping carts		
Sirens		
Skateboards		

Records

	8-12 Weeks	3–9 months
Stairs		
Statues		
Thunderstorms		
Traffic		
Trains		
Trucks		
Umbrellas		
Vacuum Cleaner		
Vending machines		
Wheelchairs		
People		
25 Women		
25 Men		
15 Teenagers		
15 Children (5-12)		
15 Toddlers (2-4)		
5 Infants (0-1)		
Arguing		
Children in strollers		
Children playing		
Crying		
EMTs		
Firemen		
In costumes		
Laughing		
Police officers		

	8-12 Weeks	3–9 months
Runners		
With beards		
With boots		
With canes		
With crutches		
With hats		
With helmets		
With hoods		
With sunglasses		
With a walker		
Surfaces		
Asphalt		
Brick		
Carpet		
Concrete		
Dirt		
Elevators		
Grass		
Grates		
Gravel		
Hardwood		
Metal		
Sand		
Stairs		
Tile		
Wobbly surfaces		

Copyrighted Information

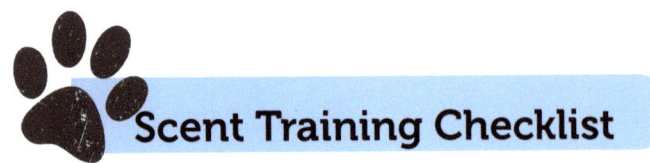

Scent Training Checklist

To ensure your dog will alert in every situation, you must practice in every situation. When you reach Step 9 of scent training, begin practicing in every scenario you can imagine. The checklist below is a great start - each time you scent train in one of these scenarios, check it off the list!

Handler Sitting

- At the computer (x10)
- Reading a book (x10)
- Watching TV (x10)
- T1D on a sofa, dog on place (x10)
- Eating a meal (x20)

Handler Laying Down

- Laying on the sofa (x10)
- In bed - to mimic night alerts (x20)

Handler Standing

- Getting ready for the day (x10)
- Cooking a meal (x10)
- Doing the dishes (x10)
- While in the shower/tub (x20)

Handler Walking

- Walking outside while raining (x5)
- Walking through the house (x10)
- Heeling around neighborhood (x10)
- Walking in the country on lead (x10)
- Walking off lead (where permitted) (x10)
- Heeling in the city (x10)
- Walking by the dog park (x10)
- Walking by a park with kids (x10)

Scent Training Checklist

Other In Home Scenarios

While playing (fetch/tug/etc.) (x5)
Dog tethered (on a leash to a chair, table, etc.,); sample ≥ 6 inches away (x10)
Dog in kennel (x10)
While practicing obedience training (x10)
At a friend's home (x10)
While chewing on a bone (x10)
While playing by itself (x10)
While grooming the dog (x10)
Outside in the yard (x20)
While playing with other dogs (x20)

Transportation

Parked car (x5)
On a train (x10)
On a bus (x10)
On a subway (x10)
Car while moving (x20)

Public

Indoor mall (x5)
Outdoor mall (x5)
Movie theater (x5)
Sports game (x10)
Home improvement store (x10)
Grocery store without a cart (x10)
Grocery store with a cart (x20)
At the office/work/school (x20)
Cafe (x20)
Restaurant (x20)

MD Dogs Verification Alert Log

HANDLER NAME: JANE DOE
DOG NAME: FI DOE

Low alert criteria	85MG/DL
High alert criteria	175MG/DO
Rapid Rise alert criteria	3MG/DL/MIN
Rapid Drop alert criteria	3MG/DL/MIN

Records

Date	Time	BG Level (Glucometer reading (not CGM))	Alert, Miss, or False	Type of Alert (Low, High, Rapid Rise, Rapid Drop)	Location (Home, Public, or Transportation)	Notes
10/1/2019	9:01 AM	125>137	FALSE		Home	
10/1/2019	9:50 AM	212	ALERT	HIGH	Home	
10/1/2019	1:32 AM	79	ALERT	LOW	Car	
10/1/2019	1:45 AM	99>126	ALERT	RR	Car	
10/1/2019	3:29 AM	65	ALERT	LOW	Home	
10/1/2019	4:13 AM	103<128	ALERT	RR	Car	
10/1/2019	4:41 AM	140>149	FALSE		Store	
10/1/2019	5:47 AM	117>105	FALSE		Home	
10/2/2019	9:10 AM	107>128	FALSE		Public	
10/2/2019	9:44 AM	116>107	FALSE		Home	
10/2/2019	9:19 p.m	74	ALERT	LOW	Home	
10/2/2019	9:36 AM	71	ALERT	LOW	Home	
10/2/2019	9:47 AM	128	ALERT	RR	Home	
10/3/2019	9:31 AM	116>79	ALERT	RD	Home	
10/3/2019	8:40 PM	168>174	FALSE		Home	
10/3/2019	9:06 PM	169>166	FALSE		Home	
10/3/2019	9:47 AM	130>102	ALERT	RD	Home	
10/3/2019	10:06 AM	93>98	FALSE		Home	
10/3/2019	11:28 AM	108>99	FALSE		Home	
10/4/2019	8:32 AM	115>109	FALSE		Home	
10/5/2019	8:41 AM	97>139	ALERT	RR	Home	
10/5/2019	1:49 AM	215	ALERT	HIGH	Home	
10/5/2019	8:20 AM	136>121	FALSE		Home	
10/5/2019	4:22 AM	81	ALERT	LOW	Home	
10/5/2019	5:34 AM	150>194	ALERT	RR	Home	
10/5/2019	6:31 AM	180	ALERT	HIGH	Home	
10/5/2019	8:11 AM	222	ALERT	HIGH	Home	
10/6/2019	12:52a.m.	111>97	FALSE		Home	

Records

10/6/2019	11:00 AM	95>101	FALSE	Home
10/6/2019	12:52 PM	89>92	FALSE	Home
10/6/2019	4:33 AM	142>88	ALERT	Home
10/6/2019	4:50 AM	92>82	ALERT	Home
10/6/2019	5:44 AM	126>137	FALSE	Home
10/6/2019	6:12 AM	151>151	FALSE	Homr
10/6/2019	7:54 AM	125>115	FALSE	Home
10/6/2019	8:43 AM	100>100	FALSE	Transportation
10/6/2019	9:09 AM	104>108	FALSE	Public
10/6/2019	9:23 AM	120>124	FALSE	Public
10/6/2019	9:42 AM	122>130	FALSE	Public
10/6/2019	11:03 AM	94>80	ALERT	Transportation
10/6/2019	11:23 AM	82	ALERT	Home
10/7/2019	9:56 AM	98>125	ALERT	Home
10/7/2019	12:15 PM	115<110	FALSE	Car
10/7/2019	2:18 AM	78	ALERT	Car
10/7/2019	4:03 AM	90>85	FALSE	Car
10/7/2019	4:18 AM	73	ALERT	Home
10/7/2019	4:26 AM	62	ALERT	Home
10/7/2019	5:40 AM	66	ALERT	Home
10/7/2019	5:50 AM	80	ALERT	Public
10/7/2019	8:01 AM	114>129	FALSE	Home
10/7/2019	8:28 AM	121>142	FALSE	Home
10/8/2019	7:48 AM	124>94	ALERT	Home
10/8/2019	8:35>8:49	129>151	FALSE	Home
10/8/2019	7:00 AM	95>84	ALERT	Home
10/8/2019	7:15 AM	89>98	FALSE	Public
10/8/2019	7:58 AM	129>143	FALSE	Public
10/8/2019	8:34 AM	138>139	FALSE	Home

	RD (row 3)
	LOW (row 4)
	LOW (row 12)
	LOW (row 13)
	RR (row 14)
	LOW (row 16)
	LOW (row 18)
	LOW (row 19)
	LOW (row 20)
	LOW (row 21)
	RD (row 24)
	LOW (row 26)

Records

MD Dogs Verification Alert Log

Handler Name: _____
Dog Name: _____

Low alert criteria		Rapid Rise alert criteria
High alert criteria		Rapid Drop alert criteria

Date	Time	BG Level (Glucometer reading, not CGM)	Alert, Miss, or False	Type of Alert (Low, High, Rapid Rise, Rapid Drop)	Location (Home, Public, or Transportation)	Notes

140 M.D. Dogs Inc. Training Your Pet To Be Your Partner

Records

Date	Time	BG Level Glucometer reading (not CGM)	Alert, Miss, or False	Type of Alert Low, High, Rapid Rise, Rapid Drop	Location Home, Public, or Transportation	Notes

Records

MD Dogs Training Log

Handler Name: JANE DOE
Dog Name: FI DOE

Record all training in a log like this to easily add up your dog's total hours of training. You can record in any way that is most helpful for you and your dog.

Date	Duration	Location	Area of training (Command, socialization, public access, etc)	Specifics (Criteria, distraction level, etc.)	Dog's performance (Scale of 1-10, # of successes, etc.)	Notes
1/1/2020	5 min	Home	Sit Stay	10 sec	9	Very good! Broke once
1/1/2020	5 min	Home	Down Stay	10 sec	9	Very good! Broke once
1/1/2020	5 min	Home	Heel	Luring	9	Very good - attempts to jump if lure is too high
1/2/2020	5 min	Lowes	Socialization	No petting, just exposure	10	Very confident, no hesitation
1/2/2020	10 min	Home	Stays and Come	10 sec stays	8	Come is excellent, began to anticipate after a few reps
1/3/2020	5 min	Home	Place	2 minute max	5	Broke place multiple times - needs work.
1/3/2020	15 min	Café	Socialization	No petting, just exposure	10	Excellent - outgoing and curious and confident
1/4/2020	10 min	Home	Heel	Fading lure	7	Jumped as soon as lure was being faded
1/4/2020	5 min	Lowes	Socialization	No petting, just exposure	10	Excellent - outgoing and curious and confident
1/4/2020	15 min	Home	Leave It	Toys as distraction	3	Needs work - very toy motivated
1/5/2020	20 min	Café	Socialization	No petting, just exposure	10	Excellent - machines were no problem
1/6/20	5 min	Home	Watch Me and Heel	Fading lure for heel	7	Fading lure is still struggle for heel. Watch me excellent
1/6/2020	10 min	Home	Place, Stays, Heel	No lure for heel; place 2 min	6	Jumped for lure, but placed for 2 min!
1/6/2020	5 min	Home	Down Stay	20 seconds	4	Broke a few times, but readily tried again.
1/6/2020	5 min	Home	Recall	10 feet	10	Very enthusiastic
1/7/2020	5 min	Home	Place	3 min and 2 min	8	Not relaxed but didn't break
1/7/2020	15 min	Home	Place	3.5 min and 1.5 min	8	Not relaxed but kept it the entire time
1/7/2020	20 min	Café	Socialization	No petting, just exposure	10	Very confident
1/8/2020	5 min	Home	Heel	No lure, 10 pace & reward	7	Pretty good; needs work on not jumping
1/8/2020	10 min	Home	Stays	Worked up to 30 seconds	9	Changed positions some but remained stationary!
1/9/2020	5 min	Feed Store	Public Access	Heel, sit, and down	7	Good for early on! Tried hard but definitely stimulated
1/9/2020	5 min	Home	Heel	No lure, 15 paces & reward	10	Very good progress
1/9/2020	15 min	Home	Leave it, heel, place, etc.	No lure for heel; place 5 min	9	A little overly enthusiastic at times but did well
1/10/2020	10 min	Lowes	Public Access	Heel, sit, down, and stays	6	Difficulty switching from in motion to stationary activities
1/10/2020	5 min	Home	Place and Heel	4 min place; no lure for heel	8	Very good - remained on place. Not relaxed but trying
1/10/2020	5 min	Home	Heel and Stays	No lure for heel; stay 45 sec	10	Excellent - no jumping for heel and stayed for 45 sec

MD Dogs Training Log

Handler Name: _____
Dog Name: _____

Record all training in a log like this to easily add up your dog's total hours of training. You can record in any way that is most helpful for you and your dog.

Date	Duration	Location	Area of training Command, socialization, public access, etc	Specifics Criteria, distraction level, etc.	Dog's performance Scale of 1-10, # of successes, etc.	Notes

Records

www.ingramcontent.com/pod-product-compliance
Lightning Source LLC
Chambersburg PA
CBHW041831300426
44111CB00002B/51